Race, Ethnicity, and the Politics of City Redistricting

SUNY SERIES IN

AFRICAN AMERICAN STUDIES

JOHN R. HOWARD AND ROBERT C. SMITH, EDITORS

RACE, ETHNICITY, AND THE POLITICS OF CITY REDISTRICTING

Minority-Opportunity Districts and the Election of Hispanics and Blacks to City Councils

Joshua G. Behr

State University of New York Press

Published by
STATE UNIVERSITY OF NEW YORK PRESS, ALBANY

Printed in the United States of America

For information, address State University of New York Press,
90 State Street, Suite 700, Albany, NY 12207

Production, Laurie Searl
Marketing, Michael Campochiaro

Library of Congress Cataloging-in-Publication Data

Behr, Joshua G., 1967–
Race, ethnicity, and the politics of city redistricting : minority-opportunity districts and the election of Hispanics and Blacks to city councils / Joshua G. Behr.
p. cm. — (SUNY series in African American studies)
Includes bibliographical references and index.
ISBN 0-7914-5995-0 (alk. paper) — ISBN 0-7914-5996-9 (pbk. : alk. paper)
1. City council members—United States. 2. Local elections—United States.
3. Apportionment (Election Law)—United States. 4. Gerrymandering—United States.
5. African American legislatures. 6. Hispanic American legislators. I. Title. II. Series.

JS371.B44 2004
320.8'5'08900973—dc22 2003060635

10 9 8 7 6 5 4 3 2 1

Contents

Tables and Figures

Tables

FIGURES

ACKNOWLEDGMENTS

I would not have been able to bring the manuscript to its current state without the loving support, and patience, of my wife, Patti. To her I owe much. I thank my daughters, Abigail and Hannah, for reminding me daily of the preciousness of life. It is difficult to pinpoint whence the thesis of a book comes. Although I did not know it at the time, the genesis must be credited to Guillermo Gomez with whom I discussed affirmative government efforts to guarantee "a slice of the pie." Through his careful words I was given some of the best education one could hope. I would like to give a special thanks to Dick Engstrom for his attention to detail and constructive comments over the years. Through the process of having to place one's thoughts on paper one is forced to confront the rationale and logic of his assertions. The process is one of self-education and revision—the work never quite complete. Recently I had the pleasure of briefly sharing time with Veda Lindsay. She gave much over the years to do good works in His name and share her love of Jesus with generations of children. Glory be to God, for great things He hath done.

CHAPTER ONE

THE CITY: STEPCHILD OF REDISTRICTING CONTROVERSIES

The 1990s were much celebrated for marked increases in the number of Hispanic and black elected officials at the state and national levels relative to previous decades. Explanations for these recent gains may include a myriad of idiosyncratic factors peculiar to particular elections, but most often cited is the central role of redistricting. There is a general consensus among perceptive public officials, political pundits, and academics alike that these gains are the result of a dynamic process that has been going on for several decades. Correctly, it has been largely asserted that these increases are the culmination of a decades-long process that includes congressional acts, federal court rulings, and affirmative efforts by the U.S. Department of Justice to realize a more representative government through the oversight of election practices, including the fundamental process of redistricting. Underpinning this dynamic process is the sociology of voting behavior, the raw politics of elected officials, and the geography of where we live and work. While no doubt there is consensus that redistricting decisions have impacted the who and how of elections, the redistricting process itself, and the electoral product of that process, remains by all measures contentious and controversial.

We begin our explanation of the election of Hispanics and blacks to city councils by first looking at the mechanics of election systems. The single-member district system has been advanced as the preferred remedy for the dilution of minority voting strength and, by extension, credited with the increases in elected minorities at the state and national levels. There has been similar attention focused on the single-member district election format and the election of minorities at the municipal level, too. Much of this focus, however, has centered on the single-member district format as advantageous to the election of minorities *relative* to the at-large (i.e., citywide) election format.[1] It has been demonstrated at the municipal level, for example, that both Hispanics and blacks are more likely to be elected in cities that use the single-member district format than cities that use the at-large election format.[2] This stems from the fact that under an at-large election format a minority population may be a numerical minority, but with the adoption of single-member districts it may constitute a numerical majority in one or more districts. By the 1990s it was more common than not for municipalities to use the single-member district election format.

Much of this influence on the election of minorities attributed to election format is predicated on individual behavior. It has been documented that racial minorities are more likely to run for office when they are a numerical majority within single-member districts (Helig and Mundt 1984, 58–59; Polinard, Wrinkle, and Longoria 1991; Karnig and Welch 1980, 86–87) and that voters, when given a choice between or among minority and nonminority candidates, tend to divide along group lines in their candidate preferences (Vanderleeuw 1990; Murray and Vedlitz 1978; Reeves 1997, esp. 76–90; Carsey 1995; Lieske and Hillard 1984; Issacharoff 1992; Williams 1990; Chervenak 1998, 218–31; Sigleman et al. 1995; Pildes 1997, 2512 n23; Browning, Marshall, and Tabb 1997; Walton 1985, 73–130; Dawson, Brown, and Allan 1999; Streb 2002, 189–96).[3] Yet the extent to which voters crossover to vote for candidates not of their group varies greatly (e.g., Bullock 1984; DeLorenzo, Kohfeld, and Stein 1997; Herring and Forbes 1994, 437–40; Vanderleeuw 1990).[4]

As evidenced above, within the last twenty years there has been much theoretical development and empirical testing of the relationship between election format and the increases in Hispanic and black elected representatives. Despite this attention, we are far from providing a thorough explanation of the presence of Hispanics and blacks on municipal councils. The simple presence of a single-member district format in itself does not necessarily assure that minority candidates will be elected. In addition, the condition of a minority group constituting a numeric majority in one or more of these districts certainly will contribute to an increased likelihood that minority candidates will be successful in bids for council seats. Clearly an explanation of the election of minorities, therefore, must necessarily be linked to an investigation of the adoption of districts in which a minority is in majority. Interestingly, many single-member districted cities with similar-sized minority populations vary in the proportion of council districts that have been adopted as majority-minority. This begs the obvious question: How may we account for these differences in seemingly similar cities? In other words, under what conditions do some single-member district format municipalities with a sizable minority population adopt majority-minority districts while others do not?

The primary argument of this book is that while many of the forces that shaped the creation of majority-minority districts at the state and national levels may also be at play at the local level, the relative intimacy of the local political process arguably provides for different dynamics. It should not be assumed that pressures exerted in state and congressional redistricting will produce the same results at the local level. This study provides an accounting of the local dynamics that may suppress the proposal and adoption of districts in which a specified minority is in numeric majority and, in turn, frustrate the election of Hispanic or black representatives. To provide this accounting, a creative and somewhat unorthodox approach has been taken. Rather than asking, "What may account for the presence of majority-minority districts?" we begin by asking, "Assuming the maximal number of majority-minority districts that are theoretically possible (based on the size of the city's total population, the minority population, and the number of seats on the council), what may account for the *absence* of majority-minority districts?" Simply, we study the variables that account for the difference between the maximal number of majority-minority council districts that are theoretically possible, independent of any other geographic or political considerations, and the number of majority-minority council districts that, in fact, have been actually adopted.

Rarely is the number of majority-minority districts actually adopted equal to this theoretical maximum. The relationship between this theoretical maximum of majority-minority districts and the majority-minority districts that are actually adopted is the first general relationship (i.e., general hypothesis 1) we investigate. This relationship is conditioned by specifying variables that reflect the real-world mechanical and political processes of municipal districting. These specifying variables are political tenability, vested minority incumbent advocacy, divested minority incumbent advocacy, preclearance, and court intervention.

The concept of 'political tenability' addresses the ability to defend or sustain, politically, proposed majority-minority districts. Majority-minority districts that can be defended as resulting from the use of districting criteria other than race, such as compactness, contiguity, respect for existing political subdivisions, or communities of shared interest, are more tenable politically. Simply, majority-minority districts are easier to sell politically if they can be defended on grounds other than race. For example, cities with highly segregated minority populations may find it easier to construct compact majority-minority districts and assert that a concern for the preservation of a community of shared interest, rather than simply race, motivated the district. However, cities with low levels of segregation may require the creation of Rorschach-shaped majority-minority districts that are less defensible on grounds other than race and, thus, less tenable politically.

On the one hand, the concept of 'vested minority incumbent advocacy' touches upon the possibility that a minority incumbent elected from a district may be involved directly in districting decisions. A minority incumbent's decision to push for the creation and adoption of majority-minority districts is qualified. The minority incumbent is likely to support the creation of majority-minority districts provided that the adoption will not threaten his or her existing electoral base by siphoning off preferred constituents into the newly proposed majority-minority districts. On the other hand, the concept of '*divested* minority incumbent advocacy' suggests that the electoral prospects of an at-large minority incumbent in a mixed election system[5] are divested from moves to create majority-minority districts. Since elected at-large, the adoption of majority-minority districts and the resultant shuffling of constituencies is not likely to directly endanger his or her electoral prospects.

The concept of 'preclearance' addresses whether a districting plan is subject to the federal preclearance provisions under the Voting Rights Act. Local redistricting officials may struggle to resist both external pressures and federal oversight that pushes to heighten the use of race as a districting criterion. Last, the concept of 'court intervention' also touches upon the breaching of the parochial municipal districting process by outside actors resulting, once again, in a heightened priority accorded to race-based districting.

The adoption of majority-minority districts, in turn, has a direct effect on the election of Hispanics and blacks to city councils. The presence of majority-minority districts does not necessarily insure the election of Hispanic or black representatives. In the second general relationship (i.e., general hypothesis 2) we investigate the elections of Hispanics and blacks from these districts in the three elections subsequent to the 1990 round of redistricting. The relationship between majority-minority districts and the election of Hispanic and black representatives is itself conditioned by the specifying variables of resource disparity, partisan elections, and district population density.

The concept of 'resource disparity' taps the importance of politically relevant resources, such as education and income, which may contribute to the level of minority electoral participation. Also, the presence of party organizations to provide official endorsements, raise money, and assist with campaigns is expected to enhance the electoral prospects of minority candidates. Last, given limited resources, the population density of council districts may influence a campaign's ability to communicate with voters either through the media or via direct in-person contact and, thus, impact the mobilization of voters.

This book argues that the presence of Hispanics and blacks on city councils is explained primarily by the adoption of majority-minority districts in which minority groups are provided a meaningful opportunity to elect candidates of choice. The question of what percent of a district's over-all population must necessarily be minority to provide the group with a "meaningful opportunity" is contentious (e.g., Epstein and O'Halloran 1999). It has been argued, for example, that a simple majority (50 percent plus 1) may not provide the opportunity for a minority community to elect a representative of its choice because "levels of African-American income, education and health [which relate to political participation] have lagged below those of whites [due to past] . . . racism and discrimination" (Zellner and Carey 1990, 68). Although the particular size that a minority must constitute within a single district in order to provide a meaningful opportunity to elect a candidate of choice may vary greatly from city to city, some voting-rights advocates have encouraged, and some courts have accepted, as much as a 65 percent overall minority population to compensate for lower levels in voting-age population, registration, and turn-out among minorities.[6] Given the absence of consensus on what may provide minorities with a meaningful opportunity to elect candidates of preference, this research examines separately the impact of districts with at least 50, 55, and 60 percent minority voting-age population, hereafter identified as minority-*opportunity* districts.

Chapter 2 explicates the two general hypotheses linking the primary variables of system aptitude (the theoretical maximum number of minority-opportunity districts allowed by a system), the actual presence of adopted minority-opportunity districts, and the presence of Hispanics and blacks on city councils. Chapter 3 develops more thoroughly the theoretical underpinnings of the specifying variables that condition the two general hypotheses. Chapter 4 offers a summary of the hypothesized relationships and detailed measures of the model's variables. Chapters 5 and 6 respectively present the findings for the model's first and second general relationships. The concluding chapter presents a brief analysis of the probability of electing a minority councilperson based on the percent of the district that is minority, a discussion of the progress made in defining meaningful opportunity, and the policy implications of our findings. The cities in this study and the type of survey instruments utilized are included in the appendices.

Attempting to explain social phenomena is risky business. Social phenomena are inherently complex, and in the process of investigation and explanation the social scientist is faced with a two-edged sword: on the one hand, by following Ockham's law and providing a parsimonious explanation, we run the risk of being accused of oversimplifying a very complex process; on the other hand, any attempt to provide a *complete* explanation must necessarily be voluminous. The art of this book, as any good social science book, is that it attempts a focused approach by investigating in depth and making tractable several important concepts while at the same time recognizing throughout the work the richness and complexity of the phenomena. While this work certainly does not claim to quell the raging redistricting debate, it does shed light on several important questions and does contribute to our body of knowledge by presenting compelling evidence of the forces that account for the creation of municipal minority-opportunity districts during the 1990 round of redistricting and the election of Hispanics and blacks in the three elections subsequent to this redistricting. Thus, the utility of this work is not found in that it satisfies most participants in the redistricting controversies, but, rather, it adds to the quality of the debate, especially at the municipal level where we believe the discussion has taken second stage to state and congressional redistricting controversies, and the dynamics have been assumed to apply to the local level. This, after all, is the mark of progress in the social sciences.

CHAPTER TWO

Making the Connection: The Links among System Aptitude, Minority-Opportunity Districts, and the Election of Hispanics and Blacks

An explanation for the election of Hispanics and blacks to city councils necessarily requires an understanding of the occurrence of minority-opportunity districts. At the most basic level, minority-opportunity districts are wholly dependent upon there being enough minority-group members residing in the city. It is for this reason that we begin our journey with a discussion that takes stock of the perhaps not so obvious, and deceptively simple, relationship between the size of the citywide minority population and the number of districts on a council.

SYSTEM APTITUDE

A prerequisite to the election of minority candidates to governing bodies usually has been the presence of a substantial minority population of voting-age. The limited population size of municipal single-member districts provides the opportunity to construct districts that substantially encompass communities of interest, especially race-based communities of interest. This has been cited as a major reason that the presence of minority representatives on city and county governing bodies tends to be much greater than it is in Congress or state legislatures (Grofman and Handley 1989a, esp. 268–70).[1]

Within any particular city, the population size of its districts is determined by the number of council seats. Generally the larger the legislative body, the fewer inhabitants within each district. Since most cities contain a relatively small minority population, the choice between a five- and seven-member council, for example, can be quite pivotal to the creation of the first minority-opportunity district. An increase in the number of council seats can lower the district population size to the point where the minority population surpasses the threshold necessary to construct the first minority-opportunity district, which in turn provides the potential to elect a single minority candidate. Alozie and Manganaro (1993) find that an increase in the size of the council does not increase the equity in representation (i.e., more proportional representation); it does, however, increase the likelihood of the presence of at least a single black or Hispanic incumbent. The creation of the first minority-opportunity district is a point of critical juncture because minority presence on the governing body is less likely without a single minority-opportunity district.

A city council with dozens of seats may provide the opportunity to elect minority representatives due simply to the fact that it lowers the size of the district poplation, but it also may lessen proportionately the impact of a single minority member's vote on public policy. It has been argued that the size of the city council may mitigate the racial threat posed by mobilized minorities, especially in cities with a large percentage of minorities. The racial threat literature views racial groups as competing in the political arena for substantive benefits that may come from the election of preferred candidates (see, e.g., Giles 1977; Giles and Evans 1985; Giles and Buckner 1993, 1996; Glaser 1994; Voss 1996; also Dawson, Brown, and Allen 1999, 24–25; Oliver and Mendelberg 2000; Orey 2000). Longoria (1996) finds that whites living in counties with high percentages of minorities are less supportive of the creation of election districts with heavy minority concentrations than whites living in counties with few minorities.

By restricting the number of seats on a council, a system may be gerrymandered not by geography but by numbers; small city councils may achieve the same dilutive effects as the use of at-large election formats (Taebel 1978, 147–48; Grofman, Handley, Niemi 1992, 106). The courts have found that even single-member district systems can be dilutive if the districts are extremely populous due to the small number of districted seats on the governing body. In *Garza v. Los Angeles Board of Supervisors* (1990) the average district size of the five-member county governing board was 1.7 million, twice as large as any other county district in the country and as populous as a dozen of the smallest states (see, e.g., Freedman et al. 1991). The fifteen-member Los Angeles City Council, on the other hand, was established in 1876 with each official representing about 250 citizens. Today, Los Angeles still has a fifteen-member council, yet each official represents nearly 240,000 citizens, the highest seat-population ratio of any U.S. city. Conditions such as these have led some to ague that "unusually large election districts" are essentially "surrogates for at-large electoral structures" (Bullock and MacManus 1990, 668).

From these understandings we should not simply assume, as many have, that any increase in the number of council seats necessarily translates into a proportional increase in the opportunity to elect more minority candidates via minority-opportunity districts (e.g., This assumption is made by Davidson 1984, 7; Bullock and MacManus 1990, esp. 670–71; Taebel 1978, 148–49; Jones 1979, 264–65). While there is an inverse linear relationship between the number of council seats and the size of the district populations, the relationship between the number of council seats and the percentage of all districts that may potentially be drawn as minority-opportunity districts is not linear. This is a critical distinction. The former addresses the *absolute* size of the district population. The later addresses the number of possible minority-opportunity districts *relative* to all districts. An absolute increase in the number of council seats may, counter-intuitive as it may seem, decrease the percentage of all districts that are possible minority-opportunity and, therefore, decrease the percentage of council seats held by minorities.

This nonlinear relationship between the number of council seats and the percentage of all districts that are possible minority-opportunity districts can be demonstrated. Assume, for example, that a city of one hundred thousand inhabitants has a 15 percent Hispanic population. Further assume, as a matter of definition, that a minority-opportunity district must be 65 percent Hispanic (i.e., about 60 percent Hispanic voting-age) to provide a reasonable opportunity to elect a Hispanic representative. A districted system with a 5-member city council means each district will contain about twenty thousand inhabitants. If Hispanics constitute 65 percent of one of these districts (i.e., thirteen thousand Hispanics within a single district), by the definition adopted here they will have a reasonable opportunity to elect a single Hispanic representative and therefore capture 20 percent of the 5-member governing body. The 15 percent citywide Hispanic population will be proportionally over-represented with 20 percent of the seats on the council.

Now assume the same city has an 8-member city council (rather than 5) and district populations of 12,500 inhabitants. This means 8,125 Hispanics must reside in a single district to qualify as a minority-opportunity district (i.e., 65 percent of 12,500 inhabitants). In this instance, Hispanics also have the numeric potential to constitute a single minority-opportunity district (but not two) and provide a reasonable opportunity to capture a single council seat. Yet the election of a Hispanic to this seat translates into capture of just 12 percent of the governing body (rather than 20 percent in the former example). An increase from five to eight seats does not result in the ability to construct an additional minority-opportunity district and, hence, the election of more than a single Hispanic representative. Rather, an increase from five to eight seats is likely to *decrease* the percentage of all districts that may be drawn as minority-opportunity and, thus, decrease the share of the governing body held by Hispanics. In this instance the 15 percent citywide

Hispanic population will be proportionally underrepresented with 12 percent of the seats on the council.

Now assume, once again, an incremental increase in this same city from eight to nine council seats. In this instance, however, we improve the opportunity for Hispanic representation by increasing the prospects of creating not one but two minority-opportunity districts. This provides the opportunity to increase the share of Hispanic-held council seats from 12 to 22 percent. The addition of a single district to the eight-member council, in this situation, increases the opportunity for the minority to achieve more than proportional representation.

The important point demonstrated is that there is not a linear relationship between the number of seats on the governing body and the relative opportunity for a minority to elect representatives of its choice by means of minority-opportunity districts. Table 2.1 demonstrates the pulse-decay function of the percentage of districts that can be constructed potentially as minority-opportunity.

TABLE 2.1

RELATIONSHIP BETWEEN NUMBER OF SEATS AND PERCENTAGE SHARE OF DISTRICTS THAT ARE MINORITY-OPPORTUNITY BASED ON 15 PERCENT MINORITY POPULATION

# SEATS	CITY POPULATION	DISTRICT POPULATION	65% OF DISTRICT	# MIN-OPP. DISTRICTS	% MIN-OPP. DISTRICTS	PERCENT RANGE*
1	100,000	100,000	65,000	0	0%	0
2	100,000	50,000	32,500	0	0%	
3	100,000	33,333	21,666	0	0%	
4	100,000	25,000	16,250	0	0%	
5	100,000	20,000	13,000	1	20%	8
6	100,000	16,666	10,832	1	16%	
7	100,000	14,285	9,285	1	14%	
8	100,000	12,500	8,125	1	12%	
9	100,000	11,111	7,222	2	22%	6
10	100,000	10,000	6,500	2	20%	
11	100,000	9,090	5,909	2	18%	
12	100,000	8,333	5,416	2	16%	
13	100,000	7,692	5,000	3	23%	5
14	100,000	7,142	4,642	3	21%	
15	100,000	6,666	4,333	3	20%	
16	100,000	6,250	4,065	3	18%	

* Range between largest and smallest percentage within each pulse-decay iteration.

Note: For the purposes of this illustration a minority-opportunity district has been defined as one in which the minority constitutes at least 65 percent of a district's total population (i.e., about 60 percent minority voting-age population).

As illustrated in the fifth column, the maximal number of minority-opportunity districts increases positively in a steplike, rather than a linear, fashion. As the number of council seats increases and the district population falls, the maximal number of minority-opportunity districts stays stable until the falling district population reaches a point at which an additional minority-opportunity district can be constructed. As illustrated in the sixth column, the *percentage* of all districts that potentially can be constructed as minority-opportunity fluctuates in a pulse-decay fashion. When the district population falls to the point at which an additional minority-opportunity district is created, the percentage of all districts that are minority-opportunity is at its zenith. As the number of council seats increases, the percentage of all districts that are minority-opportunity gradually decays only to surge upward once again. As illustrated in the far-right column, with an increase in the number of districts, the range between the largest and smallest percentage of all districts that are minority-opportunity within each pulse-decay iteration diminishes. The percentage of all council districts that are minority-opportunity fluctuates eight percentage points, between 12 and 20 percent, when a single minority-opportunity district is created, six percentage points with two minority-opportunity districts, five percentage points with three minority-opportunity districts, and so forth.

For illustrative purposes I chose a citywide Hispanic population of 15 percent, but these figures can be estimated for any size minority population. Figure 2.1 below presents these relationships for cities with black populations from 10 to 50 percent.

As illustrated in figure 2.1, there is a threshold number of seats below which not a single minority-opportunity district is feasible. For example, the ability to construct the first minority-opportunity district in a city with 10 percent citywide black population does not occur until the council contains at least seven seats based on the 65 percent minority-opportunity standard.[2] With six or fewer council seats it is mathematically impossible to create a minority-opportunity district, and a minority presence on the council is likely to be severely retarded. There is an inverse relationship between threshold and size of minority population; the smaller the minority population, the more districts are required before the minority population has the numeric potential to constitute at least one minority-opportunity district.

Second, also illustrated in figure 2.1, the creation of the maximum number of minority-opportunity districts tends to provide the opportunity to over-represent minorities on the city council. That is, once the district size threshold is surpassed and the first possible minority-opportunity district is constructed, in nearly all instances the minority has a reasonable opportunity to capture a number of seats in excess of their proportional representation. Given a 20 percent black population, for example, the maximal proportion of minority-opportunity districts, and therefore the potential percent share of the governing body held by blacks, exceeds proportional representation in all instances except for one. In fact, the minority may be overrepresented by as much as 11 percent. While the degree of overrepresentation may vary depending on the relative size of the minority population and the number of seats, the tendency toward overrepresentation itself is quite common.

FIGURE 2.1

MAXIMAL PERCENTAGE OF ALL DISTRICTS THAT MAY BE CONSTRUCTED AS MINORITY-OPPORTUNITY PROVIDED NUMBER OF DISTRICTS AND PERCENTAGE BLACK CITYWIDE POPULATION

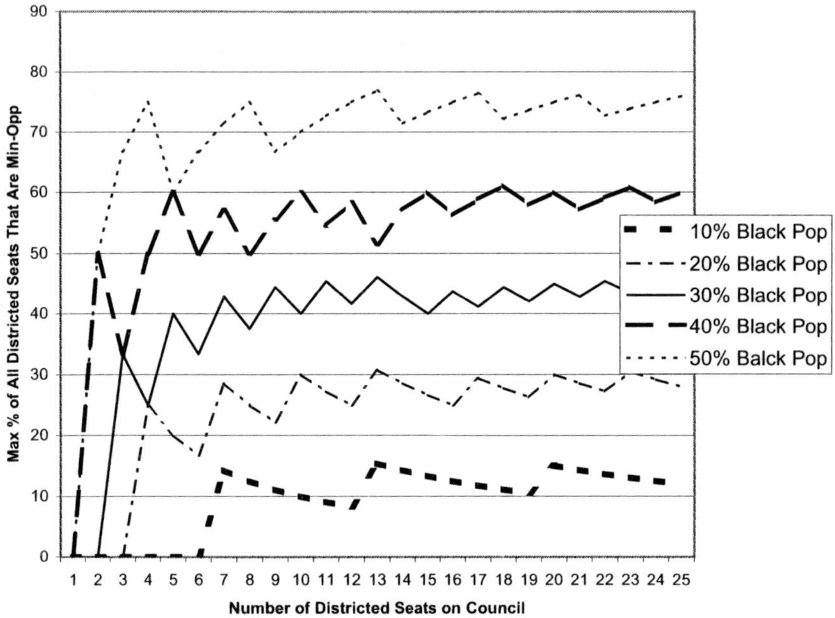

Note: For the purposes of this illustration a minority-opportunity district has been defined as one in which the minority constitutes at least 65 percent of a district's total population (i.e., about 60 percent minority voting-age population).

Third, as the number of seats increases, the range narrows in the proportion of districts that are maximally minority-opportunity. This means that as we progress toward a greater number of council seats, the addition of one or two seats has relatively little bearing on the proportion of council districts that may provide minority voters with a reasonable opportunity to elect a candidate of their choice.

The size of the council, in conjunction with the relative size of the minority population, determines this theoretical maximal proportion of all districts that potentially may be drawn as minority-opportunity districts. The aptitude of an election system refers to this theoretical maximum. Understanding the nature of an election system's aptitude to form minority-opportunity districts is an essential first step to predicting the actual proportion of a city's council districts that are minority-opportunity. The proportion of districts that are minority-opportunity, in turn, is the primary explanation for the presence of Hispanic and black representatives on city councils.

> *General Hypothesis 1*: The aptitude of an election system (defined as the theoretical maximal proportion of all council districts that may be minority-opportunity districts) provides the primary explanation for the proportion of a city's districts that are actually adopted as minority-opportunity.
>
> *General Hypothesis 2*: The proportion of a city's districts that are minority-opportunity provides the primary explanation for the proportion of districted council members that are either Hispanic or black officials elected from respective Hispanic or black minority-opportunity districts in the three elections subsequent the 1990 round of redistricting.

Thus far we are proposing an explanation for the election of Hispanic and black *representatives.* Implicit in this is that distinguishing elected officials as either "Hispanic" or "black" has meaning. Throughout this book we will refer to the election of Hispanics and blacks as descriptive representatives. The formalistic definition of *descriptive representation* pronounces a group "represented" when the governing body reflects the general character of the civil body; accordingly, a governing body "should have members to correspond to each feature" of the population (Pitkin 1967, 73; Mosher 1969; see also Burke 1999, 21–23). In this text the presence of minority council members denotes the descriptive representation of minority constituents (see Wilkinson 2000 for comment on 'minority' as a theoretical construct in the social sciences). *Substantive representation*, however, occurs when elected officials, independent of social characteristics, support policy proposals that are in accordance with the preferences of their constituents (Welch and Bledsoe 1988; Bullock 1999, 237; Whitby 1997, 5; Birch 1971; Riemer 1967; Bybee 1998, 31; Santos and Huerta 2001, 58–59). While a descriptive representative may also provide substantive representation, it is by no means assuredly so (Davidson and Korbel 1981, 1001; Pildes 1997, 253; Eulau and Karps 1977, esp. 236–41; Eulau et al. 1959; Cameron et al. 1996; Lublin 1999; Epstein and O'Halloran 1999; Mansbridge 1999).

It has been argued, for example, that representation comes from officials working actively to propel the interests of constituents; it makes little difference if the elected officials' characteristics mirror accurately the population at-large: "More black faces in political office (that is, more descriptive representation for African Americans) will not necessarily lead to more representation of the tangible interests of blacks" (Swain 1993, 5 and also 72–73 and 97; 1998, 195–99). Whitby (1997, 181) counters this by suggesting that "descriptive representation helps to promote . . . political stability by increasing [group] members' faith and trust in government" (see also Dawson's 1994 linked-fates thesis) and minority elected officials have the opportunity to legitimize and defend a group's preferences in the public policy process (NALEO 1994, vii; also Behr 2000). Szarawarski (2000, 4) finds that descriptive representatives "make the political system more democratic by remaining in close and continuing contact with members of minority communities." Further, Rogers and Friedman (2000, 35) suggest that while descriptive representatives may often offer substantive representation, they use a variety of different styles to advance minority interests, some focusing on advocating larger community concerns, while others rely heavily on the delivery of particularized benefits to individual constituents. We return to the concepts of 'descriptive' and 'substantive representation' in our concluding chapter, but suffice for now that we are explaining the election of descriptive representatives.

In closing, this chapter has outlined the two primary hypotheses of this work. Of course system aptitude does not wholly explain the number of minority-opportunity districts actually adopted, just as the number of minority-opportunity districts adopted does not wholly explain the election of Hispanic and black descriptive representatives. A major contribution of this research is the theoretical explication and empirical testing of the conditions that qualify these two general relationships. It is to these conditioning variables that we now turn in chapter 3.

CHAPTER THREE

Players in the Politics of "Selling" Minority-Opportunity Districts: Self-Serving Incumbents, the Feds, and Organized Interests

During the 1970s and 1980s many interest groups were effectively excluded from the details of redistricting due to limited access to technology. The 1990 round of redistricting saw digital data sets and powerful computer programs, able to aggregate block-level census data into district maps, made available widely to interested parties. Digital census data, when combined with any of several Geographic Information System (GIS) software packages, provided the ability to construct and submit alternative redistricting plans (Martin 1996, 69–70, 159–61; Foresman 1998, 286). Monmonier (2001, 6–7) documents the increased number of pages required to record congressional districts in the *Congressional District Atlas* as an indicator of the increasingly complex geometry of congressional districts.

The early 1990 round of redistricting was a juncture in "the rapid developments in computer hardware and GIS software [that] came together to revolutionize the technical aspects of electoral cartography" (Eagles, Katz, and Mark 1999, 6; Chrisman 1997). Hagens (1996, 320–21) documents the importance of access to districting technology during the 1990 round of redistricting in Virginia:

> At long last the legislature's monopoly on the technical capability to create districting plans ended. No longer could the legislature claim, as it had in past decades, that alternatives to its redistricting plans were technically impractical. [Private interests] were able to publish plans for the

minority that demonstrated the feasibility of alternative redistricting proposals that increased minority representation.

Weber (1995, 212) argues that technological advances in districting software "fed litigation and judicial activism" by providing "multiple actors the ammunition to sue" if they were not satisfied with the legislature's redistricting plans.

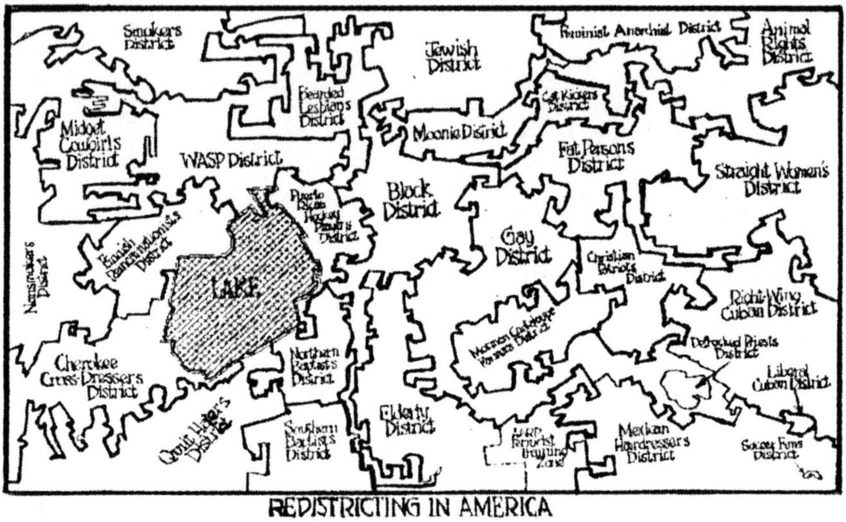

By permission of Don Wright for the Palm Beach Post

This chapter presents a discussion of the concepts that condition the two general relationships already specified in the previous chapter. Recall that the concept of 'system aptitude' is the *potential* to construct minority-opportunity districts independent of political climate or geographic constraints.[1] The technical task of drawing districting plans that include minority-opportunity districts is a relatively simple matter of mechanics given a large enough citywide minority population. The development of the variable political tenability, the first of several proposed conditioning variables, will illustrate the bridge between the *technical ability* to construct potential districting plans that contain minority-opportunity districts and the *political defense* that may contribute to either the adoption or rejection of those plans.

POLITICAL TENABILITY

The supposition thus far has been that, given a large enough minority population, a minority-opportunity district is likely to be adopted and a minority elected to office. This, however, ignores the untenable political position of districting plans that propose minority-opportunity districts with unusual or grotesque shapes. The drawing of districting plans with relatively compact minority-opportunity districts may be more easily defended or sustained politically than odd-shaped districts. Therefore, the tenability of minority-opportunity districts is dependent, in part, on the residential concentration of the minority population. While dispersion of minority population within a city may not necessarily preclude the construction of minority-opportunity districts, it often compels the drawing of Rorschach-shaped districts with fingers reaching into several scattered minority concentrations. And a relatively small number of councilmanic districts may further require the capturing of dispersed pockets of minority concentrations. Such odd-shaped districts may not be explicable on grounds other than race or ethnicity and thereby frequently raise eyebrows and lead to charges of racial gerrymandering (see, e.g., *Shaw v. Reno* 1993).[2]

People are fairly intimate with their local surroundings and generally are able to identify geographic areas within a city. These "communities" or "neighborhoods" are commonly recognized along cultural, economic, racial, or ethnic lines. This is consistent with our understanding that proximity of spatial relations is an indication of other commonalties. Simply, those living in relative proximity may share some social, cultural, political, or economic interests. According to Park, Burgess, and McKenzie (1925, 7): "Proximity and neighborly contact are the basis for the simplest and most elementary form of association . . . in the organization of city life. Local interests and associations breed local sentiment, and, under a system which makes residences the basis for participation in the government, the neighborhood becomes the basis for political control." Segregated communities are those composed of proximate individuals with shared attributes. Districting plans that cognitively do not follow commonly recognized communities may be met with suspicion and require persuasive explanation prior to acceptance.

Leaving an explanation of the actual measures of system tenability and minority segregation to the methods section to follow, it is sufficient for now to say that an extraordinarily elevated level of minority segregation means that at least 90 percent of the citywide minority population is residentially concentrated within a single area of the city and that a highly elevated level of minority segregation means that at least 70 percent of the citywide minority population is residentially concentrated within a single area of the city. A perfectly integrated minority means that 0 percent of the citywide minority population is residentially concentrated and that the minority is evenly distributed throughout the city.

To illustrate the sensitivity of the construction and adoption of districting plans to minority residential segregation, assume, for example, a seven-seat single-member district city of one hundred thousand residents, 15 percent of whom are of a particular minority. Thus, each district will contain 14,286 inhabitants. Of the city's 15,000 minorities, 9,285 (approximately 64%) must reside in one of these districts to make it a minority-opportunity district. Since the percentage of the citywide minority population that must be encompassed is less than the percent of the citywide minority population that is concentrated residentially (either 90 percent or 70 percent), districting plans may be inclusive of a minority-opportunity district that is relatively compact and that appears to be based on districting criteria other than race. A proposed plan with a minority-opportunity district that can be explained by means other than race enhances the political tenability of that plan.[3]

Now consider the same city but with a five-seat (rather than seven) single-member district system. Each of the five districts contains twenty thousand inhabitants, while citywide there are fifteen thousand minority inhabitants. The drawing of a minority-opportunity district will require that nearly 87 percent of all citywide minority inhabitants be placed into that single district. Given a highly elevated level of minority segregation, it is possible technically for cartographers to place nearly the entire minority population into a single minority-opportunity district. But this task is made difficult by the fact that, being highly segregated, only 70 percent of the citywide minority population is concentrated residentially within a single area. At best, the most compact minority-opportunity district will encompass the core segregated minority residents with fingers extending outward to capture integrated pockets of minorities. Actors in the local districting process may find the adoption of such a districting plan uncomfortable due to the overtly race-based nature of the district. In this instance, the moderate dispersion of the minority forces the drawing of a peculiar-shaped minority-opportunity district which, in turn, may raise the concern of actors necessary for the adoption of the proposed plan.

If, however, within the same five-seat single-member district system the minority is extraordinarily segregated (that is, 90 percent residentially concentrated), then placing 87 percent of the citywide minority population within a single district can be accomplished easily by cartographers and may be much more tenable politically. The creation of a single minority-opportunity district and, by extension, the ability to elect a minority-preferred candidate, is clearly sensitive to the level of residential segregation. The significant point is that the relative compactness, and therefore the political tenability, of minority-opportunity districts may be in part a function of residential segregation and the number of councilmanic districts. Whether the minority is either extraordinarily or highly segregated, the increase in the number of seats allows for the proposal of districting plans with relatively compact minority-opportunity districts that are defensible politically.

This distinction between a five-seat and seven-seat districted system in the context of either extraordinary or high segregation is illustrated in table 3.1.

TABLE 3.1

POLITICAL SENSITIVITY OF CONSTRUCTING A SINGLE MINORITY-OPPORTUNITY DISTRICT BASED ON RESIDENTIAL SEGREGATION AND NUMBER OF COUNCIL SEATS

# OF DISTRICTS	DISTRICT POP.	MINORITY POP.	MINORITY POP. ENCOMPASSED*	MINORITY RESID. SEGREGATION**	DISTRICT EXTENDS BEYOND CORE?***	POLITICALLY TENABLE?****
5	20,000	15,000	87%/13,000	70% (high)	yes	no
5	20,000	15,000	87%/13,000	90% (extraordinary)	no	yes
7	14,268	15,000	64%/9,285	70% (high)	no	yes
7	14,286	15,000	64%/9,285	90% (extraordinary)	no	yes

* Percentage/number of the citywide minority population that must be included within a single district to fashion it a 65 percent minority-opportunity district.

** High segregation means that at least 70 percent of the citywide minority population is concentrated in a single area, while extraordinary segregation means that 90 percent of the minority population is geographically concentrated.

*** Does the drawing of the minority-opportunity district require the encompassing of pockets of integrated minorities beyond the core of residentially concentrated minorities?

**** Is the minority-opportunity district explicable on grounds other than race?

Note: For the purposes of this illustration a minority-opportunity district has been defined as one in which the minority constitutes at least 65 percent of a district's total population (i.e., about 60 percent minority voting-age population).

With the addition of two more seats, the district population size drops, and the smaller district allows for the 15 percent citywide minority population to be less than extraordinarily segregated yet still concentrated enough to construct a minority-opportunity district exclusive of outlying minority pockets. Unlike the five-seat single-member district system, the construction and adoption of a minority-opportunity district within the seven-seat single-member district system is less sensitive to the level of integration, and therefore, the ability to elect a descriptive minority representative is less likely to be compromised.[4]

While some minority groups are more segregated than others, in general most minority groups are at least modestly integrated. As a minority becomes more integrated, the minimum size of the minority population necessary to construct a tenable minority-opportunity district increases.[5] The tendency of most cities to have relatively small councils, usually between five and nine seats, and to contain a citywide population that is either majority nonblack or majority non-Hispanic, increases the importance of the level of segregation in the drawing and adoption of districting plans.[6]

Figure 3.1 illustrates well the point that the tendency of city councils to be small increases the importance of segregation. An 80 percent segregated minority in a seven-seat single-member district system, for example, requires a minority citywide population of nearly twelve thousand (i.e., 12 percent in a city with one hundred thousand residents) to construct a politically tenable minority-opportunity district. Yet, if this same minority is less segregated, say 50 percent, then it must constitute at least 18 percent of the citywide population to construct a politically tenable minority-opportunity district. The difference in segregation has substantially increased the requisite size of the minority population necessary to construct and adopt a minority-opportunity district. Now compare the same 80 percent and 50 percent segregation for a fifteen-seat single-member district system. The minority must now constitute just 5.5 percent and 8.5 percent of the city's population, respectively. With an increase to fifteen districts the difference in effect between a minority being either 80 percent segregated or 50 percent segregated has been substantially diminished.

The ability to construct a second minority-opportunity district is also further frustrated by segregation. Within the seven-seat single-member district system with a 50 percent segregated minority, for example, a second politically tenable minority-opportunity district requires a doubling of minority population from 18 percent to 36 percent. A second district in a fifteen-seat single-member district system with 50 percent segregation will likewise require a two-fold increase from 8.5 percent to 17 percent. The hurdles for constructing either a first or second minority-opportunity district are manifold when the number of councilmanic districts is relatively small and the minority is fairly integrated.

FIGURE 3.1

RESIDENTIAL SEGREGATION AND MINIMUM SIZE OF MINORITY POPULATION NECESSARY TO CONSTRUCT A TENABLE MINORITY-OPPORTUNITY DISTRICT

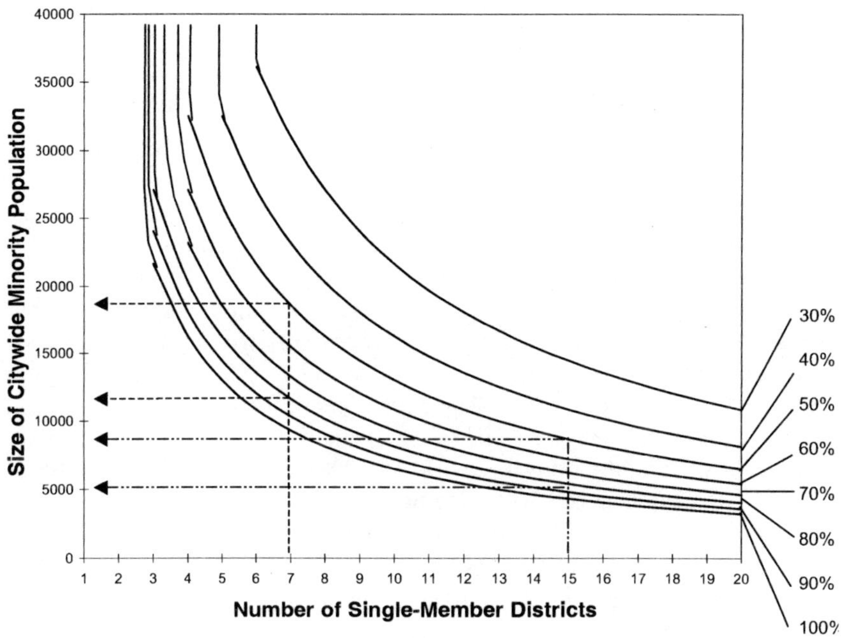

Note: For the purposes of this illustration a minority-opportunity district has been defined as one in which the minority constitutes at least 65 percent of a district's total population (i.e., about 60 percent minority voting-age population).

While it has been documented that minorities, in general, fare better in cities employing the single-member district format, it has also been demonstrated that this impact is different for blacks relative to Hispanics.[7] This is attributed, in part, to the higher level of residential integration among Hispanics than blacks.[8] Different levels of segregation between blacks and Hispanics may have a disparate impact on the adoption of minority-opportunity districts.

> *Hypothesis 3*: The variable political tenability (i.e., the ability to defend proposed minority-opportunity districts) will condition the relationship between system aptitude and the proportion of districts adopted as minority-opportunity districts. The more tenable a district, the more likely it will be adopted. Hispanic minority-opportunity districts are less likely to be adopted than black minority-opportunity districts because the greater Hispanic residential integration results in fewer politically tenable minority-opportunity districts.

The ability of a proposed districting plan to be defended or sustained is subject to the vagaries of the local political process. Council members elected from districts have a vested interest in drafting districting plans and are potentially important actors in this drama. With this in mind we now turn to two more concepts that may condition the first general relationship, vested and divested minority incumbent advocacy on the council.

VESTED MINORITY INCUMBENT ADVOCACY

Districted minority incumbency contributes to our explanation of the adoption of proposed minority-opportunity districts. Since the reconfiguration of council districts is frequently based on revisions in the existing district lines, the changes often may be incremental. Although the impact of such changes may be viewed by nonastute observers as having no consequential impact on coming elections, particular attention to these seemingly negligible adjustments to existing district lines are of particular concern to districted incumbents. According to Raskin (1995, 168), "By fencing out unfriendly voters and potential rivals, incumbents make districts in their own image and turn elections into a formality. In our self-perpetuating incumbentocracy, voters don't really pick public officials on Election Day because public officials pick voters on redistricting day" (see also Singh 1998, 107–10). Thus, districting has been likened to occurring in a Hobbesian state of nature. Issacharoff and Pildes (1996, 25), for example, assert that "redistricting in the United States has always been a nasty, brutish and self-serving power grab—a naked descent into partisan politics . . ." Golinger (1990, 45) states that prior to redistricting "sharp-eyed incumbents already have begun their survival strategies for the next decade," and Beauregard (1995, 77) admonishes, "To think clearly and effectively, we must neither ignore nor underestimate the politics of representation."

Since the drawing of district lines inherently involves choices likely to benefit some and disadvantage others, the districted incumbent legislators cannot be expected to proceed with indifference (Gronke and Wilson 1999; Ayres and Whiteman 1984, 307–08; Brown 1992; Mayhew 1971). According to Hodson (1997, 11), "legislators feel free and, indeed, compelled by self-interest and self preservation, to pursue highly idiosyncratic demands in redistricting." Making a seat more secure electorally through redistricting can be of driving concern (Bullock 1975, 571). While the particulars of a redistricting process may appear mundane, these relatively low-profile activities can have substantive consequences on the future of minorities on governing bodies.

Since the legislators themselves are often the guarantors of passage of the districting plan, their particular preferences must, to some extent, be recognized in the plan (see, e.g., Scher, Mills, Hotaling 1997, 234–35; Williams

1995, 21; Webster 1997b, 65).[9] Districted minority incumbents are likely to be elected from districts with significant minority populations, and they know that continued electoral success is dependent, to a large extent, upon the racial or ethnic composition of their districts. Behaving as incumbents, with reelection as their foremost priority, minority council members will support the maintenance, and possibly an expansion, of their own electoral base during the redistricting process, *even at the cost of additional minority-opportunity districts.*[10]

The absence of a districted minority incumbent on the council during the legislative session in which districting plans are considered is expected to contribute to a low priority accorded to race, even in cities with minority populations large enough to construct a minority-opportunity district. It is unlikely, for example, that calls for the creation of one or more black minority-opportunity districts will be heard from a council without any black members. Moreover, it should not be construed that a districted minority incumbent on the council necessarily indicates a heightened priority accorded race in the districting process. Although districted minority incumbents can be expected to be sensitive to the number of minority electoral opportunities provided in districting plans, this does not mean that minority incumbents will out of hand support an expansion in the number of minority-opportunity districts.

When, if at all, is districted minority incumbency likely to increase the priority accorded race in the districting process and, therefore, contribute to an increase in the number of minority-opportunity districts? I argue that incumbents, both Hispanic and black, are more sensitive to the electoral opportunities afforded their people than other incumbents; but this greater concern for an advancement in the number of minority elected officials is expected to play a subordinate role to the minority incumbent's vested interest in self-preservation. This raw self-interest of incumbents is echoed by Issacharoff (1997, 201):

> Through the process of redistricting, incumbent political actors choose what configuration of voters *is most suitable to their own political agenda.* The decennial redistricting battles reveal the bloodsport of politics, shorn of the claims of ideology, social purpose, or broad policy goals. Redistricting is politics pure, fraught with the capacity for self dealing and cynical manipulation. (Emphasis added)

If the construction of an additional minority-opportunity district can be accomplished without threatening the minority incumbent's electoral base, then the minority incumbent can be expected to support the additional minority-opportunity district.[11] This may be accomplished, largely, when the acquisition of additional minority council seats will not increase the respective minority's level of representation above proportionality.

For example, as a council with several districted black incumbents approaches proportional black representation, gauged as the percent of the citywide population that is black relative to the percent of the council that is black, the creation of an additional minority-opportunity district may require the transfer of black residents from the districts of existing black incumbents into the newly proposed minority district. A districted minority incumbent is not likely to support willingly the creation of an additional minority-opportunity district if it requires an erosion of his or her electoral base within his own district. In a city with a sizable council and notable black underrepresentation, districted black incumbent support for the creation of an additional minority district (or districts), near the point of proportional representation, may be more readily forthcoming. The creation of an additional minority district presumably can be accomplished without transferring large numbers of black residents out of the districts of black incumbents and, therefore, poses less of a threat to their electoral bases. Simply, districted minority incumbency combined with minority underrepresentation during the time of redistricting may increase the priority accorded to race in the districting process and, therefore, contribute to an increase in minority-opportunity districts in the new districting plan. These relationships are illustrated in table 3.2.

Support from districted minority incumbents for additional minority-opportunity districts may vary across cities that have similar levels of minority underrepresentation. This is due largely to the variation in the absolute number of council districts. Assume, for example, that there are two single-member district cities with identical 33 percent citywide black populations, one with a seven-member council, and one with a fifty-member council. Two of the seven districts in the first city are represented by blacks (29 percent of the council) and fourteen of the fifty districts in the second city are held by blacks (28 percent of the council). Based on their share of all districts, the minorities in both cities are similarly underrepresented. But the ability to add additional minority representatives to the councils and stay near proportional representation varies greatly. On the one hand, in the case of the seven-member council, an increase in minority representatives from two to three raises the minority's share of the council seats from roughly 28 percent to over 42 percent, well above proportional representation. The districted minority incumbents will be unlikely to support an expansion in the number of minority districts in this situation. On the other hand, in the case of the fifty-member council, an increase in minority representatives from fourteen to sixteen raises the minority's share of the council seats from 28 percent to 32 percent, near proportional representation. The districted minority incumbents, in this instance, are likely to support the addition of at least one or two, and perhaps three, minority districts. These relationships are illustrated in table 3.3.

Table 3.2

Incumbency and Level of Representation as an Explanation for the Expansion in Percent of Minority Districts

INCUMBENCY DURING REDISTRICTING PROCESS	THREAT POSED TO BASE CONSTITUENCY*	PRIORITY ACCORDED RACE IN DISTRICTING**	IMPACT ON PERCENT OF MIN.-OPP. DISTRICTS***
No Minority Incumbency	No	No	status quo
Minority Incumbency *and* Near Proportional Representation	Yes	No	status quo
Minority Incumbency *and* Minority Underrepresentation	No	Yes	increase

* Will the construction of one or more additional minority-opportunity districts result in a minority incumbent losing a number of minority constituents sufficient to threaten reelection?

** Will the minority incumbent contribute to a priority being accorded to race as a criterion in the districting process? That is, will the minority incumbent push for the adoption of an additional minority-opportunity district?

*** The priority accorded race will impact the percent of districts adopted as minority-opportunity districts following redistricting.

Table 3.3

Variation in the Absolute Number of Council Districts as an Explanation for Incumbent Support of Additional Minority districts

	NUMBER OF DISTRICTED SEATS	% CITYWIDE MINORITY POPULATION	NUMBER OF MINORITY-HELD SEATS	% OF SEATS THAT ARE MINORITY-HELD	PROPORTIONAL MINORITY REPRESENTATION
First City					
	7	33	2	28.57	Under
	7	33	3	42.85	Well-Over
Second City					
	50	33	14	28	Under
	50	33	15	30	Under
	50	33	16	32	Under
	50	33	17	34	Slightly-Over

When the construction of an additional minority-opportunity district may result in the overrepresentation of the minority, then support from districted minority incumbents, whether one or more, is expected to be weak. Cities with large councils and underrepresentation provide the most fertile ground for additional minority districts; cities with small councils, even those with marked underrepresentation, provide the least fertile ground for additional minority-opportunity districts since an addition will often increase representation well above proportionality. The assertion that districted minority incumbents have a vested interest in whether or not race is accorded a high priority in the districting process is well grounded in theory.

> *Hypothesis 4*: The variable districted incumbent advocacy (i.e., minority incumbency interacting with the level of minority representation) will condition the relationship between system aptitude and the proportion of districts adopted as minority-opportunity districts. If the condition of districted minority incumbency at the time of redistricting is accompanied by minority underrepresentation, then priority will be accorded race as a districting criterion and there will be an increase in the proportion of minority-opportunity districts adopted. If districted minority incumbency is accompanied by near proportional representation, then there will be no priority accorded race as a districting criterion and there will be no change in the proportion of minority-opportunity districts adopted. No districted minority incumbency implies a lack of priority accorded race and a lack of expansion in the proportion of minority-opportunity districts.

DIVESTED MINORITY INCUMBENT ADVOCACY

While the creation of minority-opportunity districts may threaten the electoral base of a districted minority incumbent, at-large minority council members within a mixed election format may find their electoral prospects largely divested from proposed redistricting changes. This should not necessarily imply that the at-large minority council members are disinterested in how districts are constructed. The prospect of the entire council enacting, or at least considering, minority-preferred policy may depend on the ability of at-large minority council members to build or expand a legislative voting coalition with other council members from the same minority group. It has been demonstrated, for example, that black legislators are more likely to "collaborate with and support other black legislators" in the sponsorship of legislation (Bratton 2001, 290). Therefore, the presence of at-large minority incumbents is likely to increase the priority being accorded to race in the districting process.

> *Hypothesis 5*: The variable divested minority incumbent advocacy (i.e., at-large minority incumbency at the time of redistricting) will condition the relationship between system aptitude and the proportion of districts adopted as minority-opportunity districts. The presence of at-large

minority incumbency at the time of redistricting will increase the priority accorded race as a districting criterion and there will be an increase in the proportion of minority-opportunity districts adopted. No at-large minority incumbency implies a lack of priority accorded race and a lack of expansion in the proportion of minority-opportunity districts.

I have demonstrated that districted minority incumbency will not, except under the condition of minority underrepresentation, contribute to advocacy to adopt minority-opportunity districts. Moreover, an at-large minority incumbent's willingness to support minority-opportunity districts is not conditioned by minority underrepresentation. These two variables assess minority councilpersons' willingness to support or propose minority-opportunity districts based on a balance between the proximate goal of maintaining one's electoral base with reelection in mind and the desire to increase influence in the legislative process through coalition building. But there also may be pressures beyond the normal dynamics of local politics that condition the adoption of minority-opportunity districts. Several of these exogenous pressures are addressed below with the variables preclearance and court intervention.

PRECLEARANCE AND COURT INTERVENTION

While local actors are the most intimately involved with the municipal districting process, there may be substantial outside influences that force a heightened priority accorded to race. External influence on the districting process may come in the form of judicial rulings, United States Department of Justice policies and regulations, congressional statutes and committee hearing reports, activities of private organizations concerned with minority voting-rights, and activities of party organizations concerned with the partisan balance in legislatures. The pressure exerted by these actors may puncture the cocoon of local districting and frustrate local political opposition to the consideration of minority-opportunity districts. The Voting Rights Act has performed an essential role in breaching the parochial process by injecting the oversight of both the federal courts and the Department of Justice. Although municipal redistricting takes place across the nation, many of these external pressures heightening the priority accorded to race are confined to particular states or regions.

It is indisputable that a struggle to define what priority ought to be accorded to race in the construction of districts has played a pivotal role in many recent redistricting disputes (see, e.g., *Thornburg v. Gingles* 1986, *Hays v. Louisiana* 1993, *Miller v. Johnson* 1995, *Shaw v. Hunt* 1996, and *Bush v. Vera* 1997; see also Grofman 1985). The drawing of district lines is not a neutral activity. The stakes are high. Different plans can advantage one minority group or partisan interest over another, or permit several "communities of interest" to remain intact while others are divided across districts (see, e.g., Shelley 1994, 190–91; Forest 1995, 98; Bork 1990, 88–89; Morrill 1987; Sauer

1918, 403–04; Monmonier 1995 and 2001, x; Rush 2000, 3–5). Any districting plan will inherently disadvantage some groups, therefore, it has been said that "all districting is gerrymandering" (Dixon 1982, 9).[12] The importance accorded to race in the districting process is of crucial importance to the formulation of districting plans. The expectation is that the greater the priority being accorded to race, the more likely minority-opportunity districts will be adopted and minorities elected. Preclearance and court intervention are two conditions that may indicate the consideration of race in the districting process.

Jurisdictions covered by the preclearance provisions of the Voting Rights Act of 1965[13] are required to have changes in any voting qualification or prerequisite to voting, or standard, practice, or procedure related to voting, approved prior to implementation. The preclearance provisions of the act, inclusive of sections 4 through 9, were targeted initially to cover only the Deep South states. The preclearance provisions were intended as a temporary measure that would apply to only state and local governments in which barriers to minority registration and voting had been perceived to be especially egregious (see, e.g., McDonald 1989, 1251–52; Stanley 1987, 94–97; Bullock and Rodgers 1975, 37).

Determination of which jurisdictions would be subject to preclearance was specified in section 4(b): Any political subdivision that "maintained on November 1, 1964, any test or device" as a condition to registration and had "less than 50 per centum of the persons of voting-age residing therein registered on November 1, 1964, or that less than 50 per centum of such persons voted in the presidential election of 1964." (With the subsequent 1970 and 1975 Voting Rights Act extensions these dates became November 1968 and November 1972, respectively.) A "test or device" was defined originally in section 4(c) to include any requirement that a person demonstrate his ability to read or write or to understand or interpret any subject matter or to be found to possess good moral character, or to be vouched for by others. The 1975 extension included provision 4(f) that expanded the definition of a "test or device." Section 4(f) states that a "test or device" was in place in jurisdictions in which more than 5 percent of the voting-age citizens were members of a "language minority" as of November 1, 1972, and which had provided registration and election materials in only the English language as of November 1, 1972, and in which less than 50 percent of the voting-age citizens was registered to vote or voted in the 1972 presidential election (28 CFR 55.5(a)(b)). A "language minority" is defined as persons who are American Indian, Asian American, Alaskan Natives, or of Spanish heritage (28 CFR 55.1). Accordingly, section 4(f) language minority jurisdictions are required to provide registration, ballots, and election-related materials in the minority language in addition to the English language and are subject to the preclearance provisions (28 CFR 55.3). The 1975 amendment identified specifically language minorities as a protected class similar to racial minorities. While many areas identified as containing a protected language minority were also areas covered previously by the preclearance requirement, most were not; the 1975 amendment expanded coverage to more than 375 nonsouthern jurisdictions (Chavez 1992, 76). The significance is that many areas outside the original southern scope are now under the preclearance provisions.

Covered jurisdictions may seek this approval from either the United States attorney general, a process called "administrative preclearance," or the United States District Court for the District of Columbia. Districting plans for cities that fall under the preclearance provisions of the Voting Rights Act must be scrutinized by either the Department of Justice or the United States District Court for the District of Columbia.[14] This is stated in section 5 of the preclearance provisions. For this reason section 5 is, for brevity, often referred to as *the* preclearance provision.

The Code of Federal Regulations identifies the submission process through which jurisdictions covered by section 4(b) and section 4(f) may acquire preclearance for a proposed change in a voting practice or procedure. Federal regulations state that the chief legal officer of a covered jurisdiction may seek preclearance from either the United States District Court for the District of Columbia, in which case the court may issue a declaratory judgment that the proposed change does not have the purpose or will not have the effect of abridging the right to vote, or from the United States attorney general, in which case the attorney general has sixty calendar days to interpose an objection to the proposed change. In practice, the submission to the attorney general is processed by the Voting Section of the Civil Rights Division within the Department of Justice where a staff attorney drafts a section 5 submission analysis and the grant or denial of preclearance comes from the assistant attorney general for civil rights acting on behalf of the attorney general (28 CFR 51.3). Although municipalities may submit redistricting plans to either the Department of Justice or the District Court for the District of Columbia, plans have been submitted to the later only infrequently. A denial of preclearance will be accompanied by an explanation for the rejection. If preclearance is denied, municipalities may attempt to assuage the Department of Justice by making the appropriate changes, often referred to as an "administrative strategy," or the municipality may choose the more costly litigative approach and submit the plan for a hearing before the District Court for the District of Columbia. Since the attorney general's decision is not subject to judicial review, the action to seek a declaratory judgment from the district court is a trial de novo (i.e., a new trial where the attorney general's previous objections are not taken into account). Although technically incorrect, this has been often referred to as an "appeal."

The purpose of the preclearance provisions is to avoid a "retrogression" in minority representation in covered areas. A grant of preclearance from the Department of Justice is dependent upon demonstration by the submitting jurisdiction that the proposed change in voting will not "lead to a retrogression in the position of racial minorities with respect to their effective exercise of the electoral franchise" (*Beer v. Unties States* 425 U.S. 130, 141, 1976; see also *City of Lockhart v. United States* 1983, *Holder v. Hall* 512 U.S. 874, 883, 1994, *Reno v. Bossier Parish School Board* 1997). This retrogression standard meant that the election plan in place at the time the jurisdiction came under the coverage of the preclearance provisions (or a plan that had received preclearance previously or was imposed by a court) would be considered the benchmark from which to determine whether any changes would be retrogressive, no matter how deplorable it was from the minority's perspective. Under these circumstances, changes to election formats that do not advance the already underrepresented minority, but maintain the status quo, may be viewed as nonretrogressive (Barker and Barker 1987, 62–63). The fact that Department of Justice review could be applied only to specific jurisdictions and substantive changes made after coming under coverage placed a formidable constraint on the preclearance provisions as a mechanism to challenge dilutive arrangements in place prior to coverage.

Section 2 of the Voting Rights Act would evolve to provide an additional protection to minorities, however. Challenges that an election system diluted minority voting strength generally fell under claims that the system violated the fourteenth and fifteenth Amendments to the Constitution as well as claims that the system violated the statutory provision of section 2. At the time of its initial passage, the section 2 provision had nearly identical language to that of the fifteenth Amendment, and it was introduced to placate southern state representatives who felt that the federal government was unfairly targeting their states for intervention.[15] Unlike the "temporary" preclearance provisions, the section 2 provision does not expire and it is national in scope, covering all state and local jurisdictions. Following passage of the Voting Rights Act, this provision initially was viewed by the courts as a restatement of the fifteenth Amendment, and therefore it was applicable only to the issue of vote denial (i.e., disfranchisement) and not to the issue of dilutive election formats.

The United States Supreme Court began to recognize by the early 1970s that certain election formats may have unconstitutional dilutive effects if they were found to cancel out minority voting strength and to provide less opportunity for minorities to elect candidates of their choice.[16] The Supreme Court did not address immediately what would specifically constitute evidence of "less opportunity." A framework for evaluating opportunity, however, came from the fifth Circuit Court of Appeals when it identified relevant factors to be considered in a vote dilution case (see *Zimmer v. McKeithen* 1973).[17] The *Zimmer* criteria remained the basis for establishing vote dilution claims through the 1970s.[18]

A sharply divided Supreme Court took what many considered a marked departure in 1980 with its ruling in *City of Mobile v. Bolden* (1980). In the *Bolden* case, plaintiffs claimed that an at-large election system diluted minority voting strength by demonstrating that the system had been detrimental to the election of minorities. Plaintiffs claimed that this constituted a constitutional violation as well as a section 2 statutory violation. The Supreme Court, however, stated that an "intent" to dilute minority voting strength, rather than a mere "result," must be demonstrated in order to grant relief under the fourteenth Amendment (see also, *Arlington Heights v. Metropolitan Housing Development Corp.* 1977). Consistent with earlier interpretations, section 2 was held to be similar to the fifteenth Amendment in that it covered questions of disfranchisement and not questions of vote dilution. According to some voting-rights advocates, the new *Bolden* intent standard was divisive in that it placed prohibitive burdens on the plaintiffs to make both a charge of and evidence of racism in the districting process (see, e.g., Reeves 1997, 95–96; O'Rourke 1992, 110).[19]

Discontent with the Supreme Court's ruling in *Bolden* led voting-rights advocates to call for legislative action. Following on the heels of the *Bolden* decision, Congress was to reconsider the extension of the Voting Rights Act's preclearance provisions that were scheduled to expire in 1982.[20] It responded by extending the preclearance provisions for an additional twenty-five years and, what is more important, by amending the section 2 provision to read that any change in voting procedures or practices "which *results* in a denial or abridgment of the right of any citizen of the United States to vote" is prohibited and that a violation occurs when members of a protected class "have less opportunity than other members of the electorate to participate in the political process and to elect representatives of their choice" (emphasis added).[21] The 1982 legislative amendments to section 2, in effect, replaced the "intent standard" with a "result standard" for evaluating claims of minority vote dilution by establishing a hypothetical, undiluted plan as the benchmark against which a proposed change or an existing plan is measured for its dilutive effect. Later, in *Thornburg v. Gingles* (1986), the Court required plaintiffs to present a hypothetical alternative to serve as the benchmark against which the existing plan is illustrated as dilutive. Hence, the section 2 results standard is unlike the retrogression standard in that the latter uses a jurisdiction's previous plan as the benchmark from which to measure retrogression. The amendments opened the way for section 2 challenges to election systems viewed as dilutive of minority voting strength. Indeed, section 2 evolved quickly into a pivotal mechanism for challenges to systems not covered by preclearance as well as for challengers to questionable plans and practices yet maintained due to the nonretrogression standard.[22]

The Senate Committee on the Judiciary released a report along with the 1982 amendments that made clear the intent of Congress in establishing a results test. The committee stated both that "proof of discriminatory intent is not required to establish a violation of section 2" and that the section 2 amendments are meant to restore "the legal standards, based on the controlling Supreme Court precedents, which applied to voting discrimination claims prior to the litigation involved in *Mobile v. Bolden*" (Senate Judiciary

Committee Report No. 417, p2, 97th Congress, 2nd Session; reprinted at 1982 USCCAN 177). The report also enumerated nine circumstantial factors that courts should examine in their totality to determine a violation of the results standard (for a summary of these factors, see Bybee 1998, 24–25). The report stated that no single or particular combination of these circumstances should be considered absolutely necessary to prove vote dilution. Subsequent district court rulings that followed the 1982 amendments failed to provide any further clarification as to the relative importance of each of these circumstantial factors in proving a section 2 minority vote dilution claim.[23]

The Supreme Court, in its first decision involving the amended section 2, provided this clarification when it identified a three-prong test necessary to establish vote dilution in multimember election formats (see *Thornburg v. Gingles* 478 U.S. 30, 50–51, 1986). Each prong of the *Gingles* test can be identified objectively, measured, and presented to the Court via expert witnesses. The first prong requires that the minority group be sufficiently large and geographically compact that it may constitute a majority in a single-member district. If the minority does not meet this test, the Court held, then the election system cannot be responsible for the minority voter's inability to elect its preferred candidates. The second prong requires that the minority be politically cohesive so that the election format may frustrate the ability of the minority to elect preferred candidates only if there is an identifiable minority interest. The third prong requires that other voters usually vote sufficiently as a block to defeat the minority's preferred candidate. In addition, *Gingles* plaintiffs also were required to demonstrate that a totality of circumstances supported the claim that the election format was dilutive.[24]

Following release of United States Bureau of the Census data in April 1991, most municipalities engaged in the districting process and implemented revised plans by 1993. The operative question becomes: During this period, what priority was placed on creating minority-opportunity districts in both preclearance and noncovered jurisdictions? The local redistricting process may have been influenced by the federal courts and the Department of Justice. On several occasions in post-*Thornburg* litigation, the federal district courts, in response to finding violations of section 2, ordered the creation of additional black and Hispanic minority-opportunity districts. But, in spite of these rulings, there was not a clear consensus among the district courts as to the circumstances under which the use of race-based districting would be either permissible or expected. The Supreme Court chose not to hear these cases, and it allowed the lower federal court decisions to stand (see, e.g., *Jeffers v. Clinton* 1989 and *Garza v. Los Angeles County Board of Supervisors* 1990).

In the early 1990s, section 2 assumed a pivotal role in heightening the priority accorded to race in the districting process for municipalities covered by the section 5 preclearance provision. Municipalities subject to section 5 were guided by Department of Justice rulings that, in many instances, directed the creation, if not the maximization, of majority-minority council districts. State and local legislators, in efforts to maximize majority-minority districts and satisfy the Department of Justice's interpretation of the 1982 amendments and federal court rulings, had cartographers with computers embark on a "search and include" approach: scouring maps, cartographers would identify pockets of minority residential clusters and couple them into one contiguous district (Engstrom 1997, 3). The Department of Justice encouraged the "imaginative cartography" of Democratic-controlled state legislative bodies, much familiar with the practices of gerrymandering (Scarrow 2000, 52).

Plans that satisfied the retrogression standard nevertheless were denied Department of Justice approval on the premise that the plans clearly violated the results test of section 2. These submitting municipalities, the Department of Justice reasoned, could have crafted plans with at least one additional minority district. This remained the Department of Justice's position through the greater part of the 1990s (Beachler 1995, 66; see also Bullock 1995, 142–43). However, in *Reno v. Bossier Parish School Board* (1997) the Supreme Court stated that these sections (the preclearance section which established a retrogression standard, and section 2, which established a result standard for the dilution of minority voting strength) were designed to "combat different evils and, accordingly, impose very different duties upon the states" (slip opinion of the Court, Justice O'Conner at part II, p.4). At question was the Department of Justice's denial of section 5 preclearance because, in its opinion, the proposed plan violated section 2 in that it was dilutive to minority voting strength. Plaintiffs noted that the Code of Federal Regulations (CFR) governing the attorney general's administration of section 5 states that the attorney general shall deny preclearance when "necessary to prevent a clear violation of amended section 2" (CFR 51.55(b)). In the *Bossier* decision the Supreme Court rejected the Department of Justice's reasoning and stated that section 5 and section 2 are distinct, and one should not be incorporated into the other. Since the late 1980s the Department of Justice had been incorporating section 2 into section 5, effectively applying the section 2 results standard to section 5 jurisdictions. The incorporation of section 2 into section 5 by the Department of Justice gave many covered municipalities an incentive to maximize the number of meaningful minority-opportunity districts to avoid both Department of Justice rejection and costly section 2 litigation.

Katherine Butler was prescient when, in a 1984 article, she suggested the preclearance provision was potentially the attorney general's most coercive tool. She noted that "in actual practice the attorney general objects to newly enacted election laws on other bases . . . [that are] . . . not subject to judicial review and can be overturned only through a burdensome declaratory judgment action in the District Court for the District of Columbia—a remedy not often pursued" (1984, 28). She claimed that armed with the preclearance mechanism the attorney general presents a "menacing specter" to cities proposing changes (1984, 42).

Many section 5-covered jurisdictions with a large minority population engaged in the 1990 process of redistricting with an "understanding that they would have to create majority-minority districts to have their plans *successfully navigate legal hurdles*" (Webster 1997a, 15, emphasis added). The complexity of voting-rights litigation almost assures substantial attorney costs. In order to encourage those who have suffered harm to seek redress in vote discrimination cases the courts have allowed plaintiffs to have attorney fees covered by the offending jurisdictions, even if the case is settled prior to trial (Scher, Mills, Hotaling 1997, 184–85).

While the Department of Justice precleared numerous plans that did not maximize, let alone increase, the number of minority districts, it was widely asserted that it had a "maximization policy."[25] Certainly, during the early 1990s, the knowledge that the Department of Justice *may* reject a districting plan for failure to construct additional minority districts combined with the submitting jurisdiction's desire to avoid potential litigation was enough to encourage race-based districting.[26] During the 1990 round of redistricting, section 5 played a pivotal role in increasing the number of minority districts precisely because it was in these areas that the Department of Justice, on numerous occasions, made preclearance dependent upon meeting the section 2 vote dilution standard. It was only later that the Supreme Court declared that the Department of Justice had erred in forcing some states to use race as the predominate factor in drawing districts (see *Miller v. Johnson* 1995).

As intended in the original Voting Rights Act and its subsequent amendments, changes in election practices or procedures proposed by covered jurisdictions are to receive heightened scrutiny. According to Butler (1984, 56–57), the preclearance requirement

> forces legislators who might be disinterested in, callous towards, or just plain ignorant of the impact of election laws on minorities to give the matter careful consideration. The existence of section 5, therefore, is a source of internal pressure on legislators to give the same serious political considerations to the impact of proposed voting legislation on minorities that they will naturally give their other constituents.

Municipalities that are covered by the preclearance provisions may not engage in the process of redistricting insulated from outside scrutiny.[27] In fact, the federal regulations governing the Department of Justice's administration of the preclearance provisions require that submitting jurisdictions facilitate minority access to the districting process.[28] Preclearance coverage subjects the redistricting process to both internal pressure and external scrutiny, which results in heightened priority for race-based districting.[29]

The impact of section 2 was more muted in jurisdictions not subject to preclearance. At the time of the 1990 round of redistricting, these municipalities were not prone to base districting decisions on perceptions of Department of Justice policy distilled from Department of Justice rulings. They were less likely to construct, much less maximize, minority-opportunity councilmanic districts. In addition, guidance as to the relative priority accorded race in the districting process was either conflicting, as was the case with district court decisions, or nearly absent, as was the case with the Supreme Court.[30] Further, section 2 challenges to their plans required a costly lawsuit in which the plaintiffs would have the burden to demonstrate, under the "totality of circumstances," that a plan had the effect of diluting the minority's voting strength. The threat of litigation under section 2 in these jurisdictions was not nearly as immediate as Department of Justice preclearance review of covered jurisdictions. Municipalities that lost or settled section 2 litigation in the decade prior to the 1990 round of redistricting, however, could be expected to be more likely to construct plans that provided minorities the opportunity to elect candidates of choice in proportion to their population than those not engaged in such litigation.

The involvement of the Department of Justice and/or the U.S. District Court for the District of Columbia in the process of preclearing districting plans, or the occurrence of litigation under section 2 in noncovered areas, signals a breach in the insulated local districting process, an increase in the priority being accorded to race-based districting, and an increase in the adoption of minority-opportunity districts.

> *Hypothesis 6*: The variable preclearance (i.e., the involvement of the Department of Justice and/or the U.S. District Court for the District of Columbia in the process of preclearing districting plans) will condition the relationship between system aptitude and the proportion of districts adopted as minority-opportunity districts. Section 4(b) jurisdictions subject to section 5 preclearance are more likely to adopt black minority-opportunity districts than those jurisdictions not included in section 4(b) coverage. Section 4(f) Hispanic heritage language minority jurisdictions subject to section 5 preclearance are more likely to adopt Hispanic minority-opportunity districts than those jurisdictions not included in section 4(f) coverage.

> *Hypothesis 7*: The variable court intervention (i.e., lost or settled section 2 litigation in the decade prior to the 1990 round of redistricting) will condition the relationship between system aptitude and the proportion of districts adopted as minority-opportunity districts. Jurisdictions with the experience of court intervention are more likely to adopt minority-opportunity districts than those jurisdictions that have not had this experience.

The above hypotheses model specifying variables that condition the first general relationship between the theoretical maximal proportion of minority-opportunity districts (i.e., system aptitude) and the actual proportion of minority-opportunity districts adopted. The second general relationship addresses the effect these adopted minority-opportunity districts have, in turn, on the presence of Hispanic and black council members elected from these districts during the three elections subsequent to the 1990 redistricting. This second general relationship is conditioned by the specifying variables resource disparity, partisan elections, and district population density.

RESOURCE DISPARITY

In low-profile elections the importance of campaign expenditures is substantial (Gierzynski and Breaux 1991). A minority group's deficit in resources relative to the nonminority group may frustrate a minority candidate's ability to raise money, achieve exposure, and mobilize voters. Talent, time, and money within the minority community, including minority-owned businesses and fraternal organizations, are necessary for effective political mobilization (Karnig 1979; Johnson 2000). Increased levels of education (Jones 1979; Robinson and Dye 1978) and income (Jones 1979; Karnig 1976; Karnig 1979; Robinson and Dye 1978) have a positive influence on many forms of electoral participation, including voter registration, voter turnout, and candidacy (especially Karnig and Welch 1980, 88–89). Therefore, education and income may be viewed as political resources that contribute to the election of minority candidates (Latimer 1979).[31] A drop in the per-capita income of the minority group relative to the nonminority group will diminish its ability to effectively mount a campaign and elect a descriptive representative.

> *Hypothesis 8*: The variable resource disparity will condition the relationship between the proportion of districts adopted as minority-opportunity districts and the proportion of council members that are either Hispanic or black officials elected from respective Hispanic or black minority-opportunity districts in the three elections subsequent the 1990 round of redistricting. As disparity in politically relevant resources increases, the ability to elect minority descriptive representatives decreases.

PARTISAN ELECTIONS

Partisan elections at the municipal level may enhance the election of minority candidates (Banfield and Wilson 1963; Hawley 1973; Robinson and Dye 1978). First, party organizations can actively recruit and train minority candidates. Political parties may contribute technical, managerial, and organizational skills necessary for effective campaigning. Political parties are institutions that certify minority candidates as eligible to receive votes of party members, and they help provide visibility through coverage by the media (Conyers and Wallace 1976, 103; Johnson 2002, 88).

Second, partisan elections allow the selection to be framed in terms of party competition and issues rather than the race of the candidate. In the absence of a partisan cue, voters will rely on other cues to arrive at their decisions (Pomper 1966). Ethnicity or race may stand in lieu of partisanship as an efficient short-cut (Squire and Smith 1988). In addition, voting cues may be expected to have the greatest impact on groups that are resource deficient or the least organized (Davidson and Korbel 1981; Lee 1960, 165–68). Without the short-cut of party cues, the cost of making decisions may increase, especially for those groups that are less informed. Partisan elections, by reducing the cost of making informed decisions, also can have the effect of increasing voter turnout (Schaffner, Streb, and Wright 2001; Conway 1969, 428).

Last, political parties may function to unite diverse community, business, and social interests in support of the sponsored candidate. This may include coordinating group members in efforts to raise money, distribute literature, staff phone banks, and register voters (White and Shea 2000, 195–97). Also, political parties may be instrumental in mobilizing voters on election day, especially those from minority communities with traditionally lower voter turnout relative to nonminorities.

> *Hypothesis 9*: The variable partisan elections will condition the relationship between the proportion of districts adopted as minority-opportunity districts and the proportion of council members that are either Hispanic or black officials elected from respective Hispanic or black minority-opportunity districts in the three elections subsequent the 1990 round of redistricting. The absence of partisan elections will decrease the ability to elect minority candidates.

DISTRICT POPULATION DENSITY

The ability of a minority candidate's campaign to both communicate with voters during the preelection period and to mobilize voters on election day may be subject to the physical density of the population within the minority-opportunity district. Generally, the larger the district geographically, the fewer voters per square mile. The more spread out the potential voters, the more organized and better financed a campaign must be to be effective (e.g., Karnig and Welch 1982, 99; Grofman, Handley, and Niemi 1992, 106; Hogan 2001). Likewise, in a more densely populated district, the minority candidate may have both more visibility and direct contact with potential voters. Simply, a high district density may increase the ability to communicate the campaign's message and to mobilize voters. Therefore, variation in population density per square mile of minority-opportunity district, weighted for the overall population size of the city, may further intensify any minority disadvantage in the distribution of politically relevant resources.

> *Hypothesis 10*: The variable district population density will condition the relationship between the proportion of districts adopted as minority-opportunity districts and the proportion of the council members that are either Hispanic or black officials elected from respective Hispanic or black minority-opportunity districts in the three elections subsequent the 1990 round of redistricting. As district density decreases, the ability to elect minority descriptive representatives decreases.

Chapter 3 has presented the theoretical underpinnings of the two general hypotheses and the attendant conditioning variables. We now turn in the next chapter to a summary of these hypotheses and the operationalization of the variables.

CHAPTER FOUR

The Design: Review of Hypothesized Relationships, Data Sources, and Measurement of Variables

This chapter begins with a summary of the hypotheses developed in chapters 2 and 3 and an illustrative diagram of these relationships. These are followed by a discussion of the data sources. The latter half of this chapter provides a detailed account of the empirical measure for each variable.

The following is a summary of hypothesized relationships:

General Hypothesis 1: The aptitude of an election system (defined as the theoretical maximal proportion of all council districts that may be minority-opportunity districts) provides the primary explanation for the proportion of a city's districts that are actually adopted as minority-opportunity.

General Hypothesis 2: The proportion of a city's districts that are minority-opportunity provides the primary explanation for the proportion of districted council members that are either Hispanic or black officials elected from respective Hispanic or black minority-opportunity districts in the three elections subsequent the 1990 round of redistricting.

Hypothesis 3: The variable political tenability (i.e., the ability to defend proposed minority-opportunity districts) will condition the relationship between system aptitude and the proportion of districts adopted as minority-opportunity districts. The more tenable a district, the more likely it will be adopted. Hispanic minority-opportunity districts are less likely to be adopted than black minority-opportunity districts because the greater Hispanic residential integration results in fewer politically tenable minority-opportunity districts.

Hypothesis 4: The variable districted incumbent advocacy (i.e., minority incumbency interacting with the level of minority representation) will condition the relationship between system aptitude and the proportion of districts adopted as minority-opportunity districts. If the condition of districted minority incumbency at the time of redistricting is accompanied by minority underrepresentation, then priority will be accorded race as a districting criterion, and there will be an increase in the proportion of minority-opportunity districts adopted. If districted minority incumbency is accompanied by near proportional representation, then there will be no priority accorded race as a districting criterion, and there will be no change in the proportion of minority-opportunity districts adopted. No districted minority incumbency implies a lack of priority accorded race and a lack of expansion in the proportion of minority-opportunity districts.

Hypothesis 5: The variable divested minority incumbent advocacy (i.e., at-large minority incumbency at the time of redistricting) will condition the relationship between system aptitude and the proportion of districts adopted as minority-opportunity districts. The presence of at-large minority incumbency at the time of redistricting will increase the priority accorded race as a districting criterion, and there will be an increase in the proportion of minority-opportunity districts adopted. No at-large minority incumbency implies a lack of priority accorded race and a lack of expansion in the proportion of minority-opportunity districts.

Hypothesis 6: The variable preclearance (i.e., the involvement of the Department of Justice and/or the U.S. District Court for the District of Columbia in the process of preclearing districting plans) will condition the relationship between system aptitude and the proportion of districts adopted as minority-opportunity districts. Section 4(b) jurisdictions subject to section 5 preclearance are more likely to adopt black minority-opportunity districts than those jurisdictions not included in section 4(b) coverage. Section 4(f) Hispanic heritage language minority jurisdictions subject to section 5 preclearance are more likely to adopt Hispanic minority-opportunity districts than those jurisdictions not included in section 4(f) coverage.

Hypothesis 7: The variable court intervention (i.e., lost or settled section 2 litigation in the decade prior to the 1990 round of redistricting) will condition the relationship between system aptitude and the proportion of districts adopted as minority-opportunity districts. Jurisdictions with the experience of court intervention are more likely to adopt minority-opportunity districts than those jurisdictions that have not had this experience.

Hypothesis 8: The variable resource disparity will condition the relationship between the proportion of districts adopted as minority-opportunity districts and the proportion of council members that are either Hispanic or black officials elected from respective Hispanic or black minority-opportunity districts in the three elections subsequent to the 1990 round of redistricting. As disparity in politically relevant resources increases, the ability to elect minority descriptive representatives decreases.

Hypothesis 9: The variable partisan elections will condition the relationship between the proportion of districts adopted as minority-opportunity districts and the proportion of council members that are either Hispanic or black officials elected from respective Hispanic or black minority-opportunity districts in the three elections subsequent to the 1990 round of redistricting. The absence of partisan elections will decrease the ability to elect minority candidates.

Hypothesis 10: The variable district population density will condition the relationship between the proportion of districts adopted as minority-opportunity districts and the proportion of the council members that are either Hispanic or black officials elected from respective Hispanic or black minority-opportunity districts in the three elections subsequent to the 1990 round of redistricting. As district density decreases, the ability to elect minority descriptive representatives decreases.

These hypothesized relationships are modeled in figure 4.1 below.

The two primary sources are data collected by means of several original surveys of city officials conducted by the author and data collected from the U.S. Census Bureau. First, data have been compiled from two surveys of U.S. cities with 1990 populations of 150,000 or more employing the single-member district election format either exclusively or in conjunction with at-large elections (i.e., a "mixed" system). Not all such cities with 150,000 population are included, however. Our theory suggests that cities that do not have enough either Hispanic or black voting-age residents theoretically to construct at least a single Hispanic or black minority-opportunity district at the 50 percent VAP (i.e., voting-age population) threshold are to be excluded (See appendix B for a list of cities surveyed). The establishment of an artificial bar excluding cities with fewer than, say, 5, 10, 12, or 15 percent minority population would be atheoretical. Other studies include such arbitrary decision rules that exclude cities with relatively small minority populations (see, e.g., Karnig 1979, 138; Karnig and Welch 1979, 465; also Taebel 1978, 144). In this study the decision to either include or exclude a city is a function of the number of both specified minority and nonspecified minority voting-age residents citywide and the number of councilmanic districts. The result of the total number of citywide voting-age residents being divided by the number of districts is the average number of voting-age residents per district. The specified minority group, either Hispanic or black, must have enough total voting-age population to constitute at least 50 percent voting-age population of a theoretical district. Thus, a city with 12 percent specified minority voting-age population may be included while another with the same percent may be excluded.[1]

FIGURE 4.1

ILLUSTRATION OF HYPOTHESIZED RELATIONSHIPS

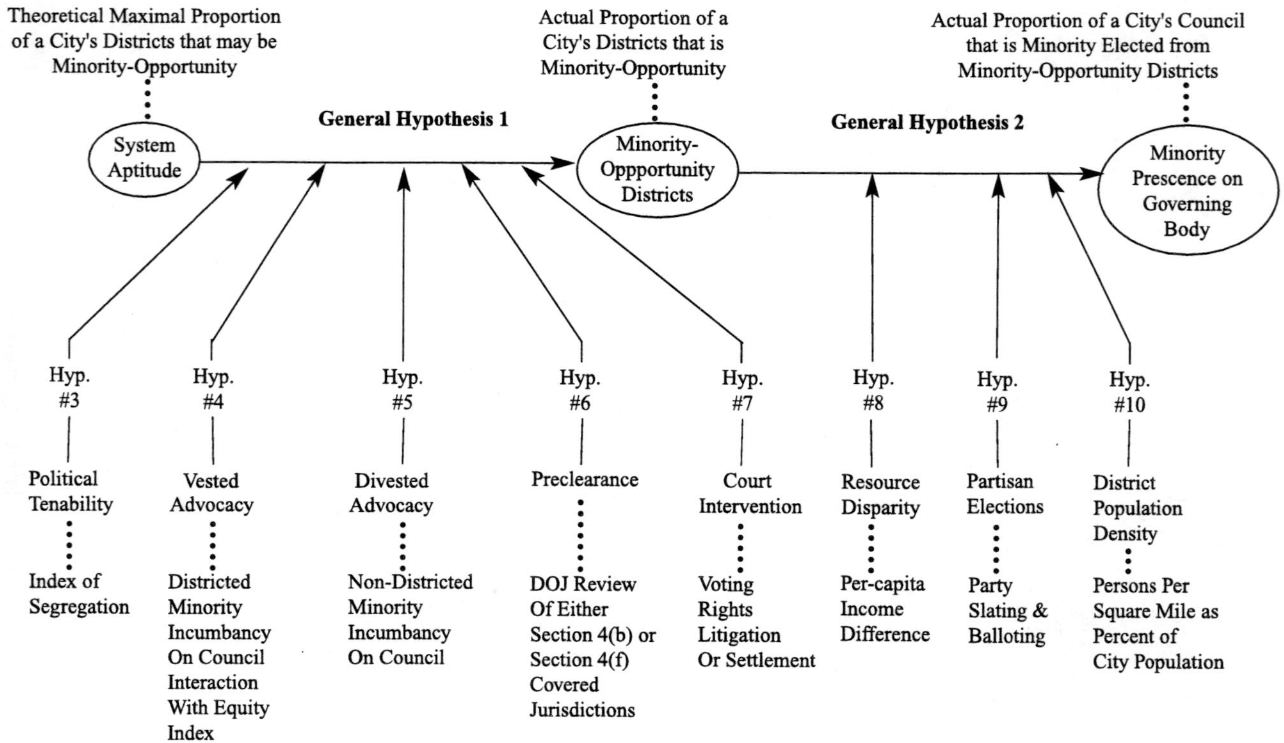

In addition, there are both theoretical and empirical reasons for us to exclude cities with an excessively large specified minority voting-age population. The exclusion of cities in which a high percentage of overall voting-age population is of a specified minority is justified on theoretical grounds. In such cities redistricters cannot avoid the proposition or adoption of minority-opportunity districts. For example, given a city with five districts and 90 percent of the overall voting-age population from a specified minority, the theoretical percent of the city's districts that may be minority-opportunity is certain to be 100, and the percent of districts that are actually adopted as minority-opportunity is likely to be 100. Thus, the translation from theoretical to actual is likely to be one-to-one. From an empirical perspective, it has been found that such a city constitutes an outlier that "tugs-up" on the regression line, substantially changing the slope coefficient and intercept relative to when the city is absent from the analysis. Further, hypothesized conditioning variables such as political tenability (i.e., segregation) will make little difference in such a city. Neither high nor low levels of segregation will change the likelihood that a proposed districting plan is attacked as motivated by race. Since all districts must necessarily be minority-opportunity, the ability of redistricters to politically "sell" a particular plan will rest on merits other than whether or not it was motivated solely by race. Those cities surveyed with the highest Hispanic VAP are Laredo with 92 percent, Miami with 65 percent, El Paso with 65 percent, and San Antonio with 51 percent. The city of Laredo has been excluded from the study for both the above theoretical and empirical reasons. Miami, El Paso, and San Antonio remain in the study. These remaining Hispanic cities do not necessarily have a system aptitude of 100 percent at all VAP threshold levels, and, in each instance, there are nonminority-opportunity districts. A check has demonstrated that these cities are not outliers empirically. Note also that these cities may have a minority *citizen* VAP (CVAP) that is lower than the standard census voting-age population (the Census Bureau reports CVAP for cities, but it does not provide these data aggregated at the block level). Thus, the VAP in these cities may actually oversate the presence of Hispanics eligible to register to vote. Those cities surveyed with the highest black VAP are the District of Columbia with 61 percent, Atlanta with 61 percent, Birmingham with 58 percent, Newark with 57 percent, New Orleans with 56 percent, Baltimore with 55 percent, Inglewood with 53 percent, and Jackson with 50 percent. Each of these cities remains in the study. These cities do not necessarily have a system aptitude of 100 percent and there are no cities that have adopted 100 percent of their districts as black minority-opportunity. Last, a check has demonstrated that these cities are not outliers empirically.

The explanation for the presence of Hispanic elected officials will employ a different set of cities than the explanation for the presence of black elected officials. This is due to the fact that often cities that contain enough Hispanic VAP to be included in the Hispanic sample do not also contain enough black

VAP to be included in the black sample. Some cities, however, have enough blacks and Hispanics to be included in both samples.

Mail, fax, and phone surveys were used to identify minority elected officials, whether they were elected at-large or to a particular district and when they held office (i.e., during the 1990 round of redistricting, during the first, second, or third election following redistricting).[2] A survey also was employed to identify cities that had been engaged in litigation prior to redistricting. See appendix A for survey design and sample of typical questionnaires.

Data are also drawn from the 1990 U.S. Bureau of the Census counts for Hispanics and blacks at the block level found in the census PL 94–171 data base and Summary Tape File 1 (STF-1). These data are used to construct measures of Hispanic and black segregation, district population density, and system aptitude. Other census data are used to measure resource disparity. Table 4.1 presents a list of variables and the attendant source of data.

The following presents the operational definitions of the variables:

SYSTEM APTITUDE

System aptitude is the theoretical maximal proportion of a city's total districts that may be either Hispanic or black minority-opportunity under the specified minority VAP thresholds of 50, 55, and 60 percent.

MINORITY-OPPORTUNITY DISTRICTS

A minority-opportunity district is the proportion of a city's total districts adopted, following the 1990 round of redistricting, as either Hispanic or black minority-opportunity under the specified minority VAP thresholds of 50, 55, and 60 percent. To determine which, if any, of a city's districts is minority-opportunity Geographic Information Systems (GIS) software is used to juxtapose a city's councilmanic district map over block-level census data. Each district's VAP by race and ethnicity is aggregated.

POLITICAL TENABILITY

Political tenability is a measure of Hispanic/white or black/white dissimilarity in residential patterns. The operationalization of political tenability is accomplished by the index of dissimilarity, measuring the eveness or dispersion of groups across the city.

The index of dissimilarity's measure of evenness has long been a staple within the sociology literature (see, e.g., Duncan and Duncan 1955; Taeuber and Taeuber 1965; Sørensen, Taeuber, and Hollingsworth 1975; White 1986, 198–89, 1987, 86–87).[3] According to Massy and Denton (1993, 20): "Evenness is defined with respect to the racial composition of the city as a whole. If a city is 10 percent black, then an even residential pattern requires that every neighborhood be 10 percent black and 90 percent white . . . The

TABLE 4.1

VARIABLES AND DATA SOURCES

VARIABLE:	DATA SOURCE:
SYSTEM APTITUDE	Survey City Clerk/Clerk of Council and Census Data Manipulated with Geographic Information Systems (GIS) Software.
MINORITY-OPPORTUNITY DISTRICTS	City's Map of Districted Councilmanic Boundaries Juxtaposed on Census Data Using Geographic Information Systems (GIS) Software.
POLITICAL TENABILITY Index of Segregation	 Census Data Manipulated with Geographic Information Systems (GIS) Software.
VESTED MINORITY INCUMBENT ADVOCACY Minority Incumbency (Districted)	 Survey City Clerk/Clerk of Council and Various Rosters of Elected Officials.
Underrepresentation	Survey City Clerk/Clerk of Council, Census, and Various Rosters of Elected Officials.
DIVESTED MINORITY INCUMBENT ADVOCACY Minority Incumbency (At-Large)	 Survey City Clerk/Clerk of Council and Various Rosters of Elected Officials.
PRECLEARANCE Section 4 (b) Covered Jurisdictions Section 4 (f) Covered Jurisdictions	 Code of Federal Regulations. Code of Federal Regulations.
COURT INTERVENTION Section 2 Litigation	 Survey Law Department/City Attorney.
MINORITY PRESENCE ON GOVERNING BODY 1st Election	 Survey City Clerk/Clerk of Council and Various Rosters of Elected Officials.
2nd Election	Survey City Clerk/Clerk of Council and Various Rosters of Elected Officials.
3rd Election	Survey City Clerk/Clerk of Council and Various Rosters of Elected Officials.
RESOURCE DISPARITY	Census.
PARTISAN ELECTIONS	Survey City Clerk/Clerk of Council.
DISTRICT POPULATION DENSITY	Census Data Manipulated with Geographic Information Systems (GIS) Software.

index of dissimilarity gives the percent of blacks that would have to move to achieve an 'even' residential pattern." A dissimilarity score of 100 indicates complete disjunction where no single person of the first group is located in areas with persons of the second group, while a score of 0 indicates complete evenness. It may be interpreted as "the percentage of non-overlap or *dis*similarity in the two residential distributions" (Sørensen, Taeuber, and Hollingsworth 1975, 127).

The index of dissimilarity, therefore, is the average deviation of a group's population size for a set of areal units within a city, weighted for the population size of the areal unit and divided by the average total population deviation. This study uses PL94–171 census block data for each city to compute a dissimilarity score. The index of dissimilarity is calculated as:

$$D_{G1G2} = \frac{1}{2} \Sigma \mid G1i/G1 - G2i/G2 \mid$$

where D_{G1G2} represents the summary statistic of dissimilarity between the two groups. G1 is the entire citywide population of the first group, and G2 is the entire citywide population of the second group. A group's population within a serial order of census tracts is designated as the *i*th tract. G1i is the population of the first group in the ith tract, and G2i is the population of the second group in the corresponding ith tract.

The index of dissimilarity has been criticized for its inability to incorporate the *spatial* relationships of geographic units, however. Assume, for example, that the census tracts within a city are arranged in red-black checkerboard fashion. Further assume that the red squares illustrate tracts that are heavily populated by whites and that the black squares illustrate tracts that are heavily populated by Hispanics. Provided this, one may calculate the city's dissimilarity index score. A shuffling or rearrangement of the location of the tracts will not alter the evenness of the racial composition of the tracts. Even if all squares (i.e., tracts) of one color are congregated on one side of the board (i.e., city) the dissimilarity index score will remain the same. But a city with tracts arranged with alternating white-dominated/Hispanic-dominated neighborhoods is qualitatively different from a city where the tracts dominated by a particular group are located largely in one or two larger clusters forming racial ghettos (e.g., White 1983, 1010–11). The failure of the dissimilarity index to incorporate a measure of the spatial clustering of areal units is known as the checkerboard or contiguity problem (see, e.g., Lieberson and Carter 1982). Since segregation is a phenomenon known largely at the neighborhood level, when a unit of analysis such as the census tract (or larger) is used to calculate an index of dissimilarity it may be subject to the checkerboard problem, and, thus, the higher level of aggregation may mask meaningful segregation. This is referred to as "scale dependency" (Beneson and Omer 2002, 13). The smallest unit of analysis, the census block, while not completely immune, is less subject to the checkerboard problem stemming from the larger-level phenomenon of neighborhood segregation. For this reason, this study uses block level census data to calculate the index of dissimilarity. (For a measure of spatial proximity or clustering see White 1983, 1986, 1987; see also Massey and Denton 1988b, 294–95; 1989, 375.)

The 1990 census provides several possible units of analysis, including the census block, census-block group, and census tract. The census block is the smallest unit of analysis and typically contains fewer than one thousand persons. The population of blocks can range from more than a thousand in areas with high-occupancy apartments to less than eighty persons. The census bureau may suppress data on race due to the relatively small size of certain city blocks and the desire to maintain respondents' confidentiality. Census-block groups average roughly forty blocks within each group, although the number of blocks may vary quite a bit. The census tract contains an average population of four thousand persons, but can range as low as three thousand and as high as eight thousand persons. The relative size of the census tract "may mask the intricacies of ethnic distributions and may be less homogeneous internally than is perhaps assumed, especially in transition zones" between segregated groups (Allen and Turner 1995, 344). The census bureau does not have a functional definition of census tract per se, although they are "designed to be homogenous [neighborhoods] with respect to population characteristics, economic status and living conditions" (U.S. Bureau of the Census, 1990 Census of Population and Housing, Washington D.C.: Government Printing Office, 1992). White (1987, 2) notes that sociologists are far from agreement on a definition for *neighborhood* and that it "is a term at once common and vague." Although many census tract boundaries have remained stable for decades, population movement as well as changes in land use have left many tracts less than homogeneous (see Rae 2001). Therefore, for these reasons it is sensible that this study uses the census block as the unit in the measure of residential segregation. (For a discussion of the evolution of PL94–171, see Turner and LaMacchia 1999).

VESTED MINORITY INCUMBENT ADVOCACY

While the complete absence of a districted minority presence at the time of redistricting may indicate that race may not be a salient districting criterion, districted minority presence is not necessarily indicative of a heightened sensitivity to race. Only when districted minority incumbency is accompanied by minority underrepresentation is there likely to be an increase in the priority accorded race as a districting criterion. Therefore, a simple dichotomous presence or absence of one or more districted minority incumbents is not adequate. Rather, the presence of districted minority incumbency, whether one or more, at the time of redistricting interacts with the number of seats required for the minority to reach proportional representation.

The operationalization of vested minority incumbent advocacy includes the interaction between two variables, the presence of districted minorities on the council at the time of redistricting and the level of minority over or underrepresentation. The presence of minorities on the council is measured as a proportion of all districts that are held by a specified minority at the time of redistricting.

The level of minority over- or underrepresentation is measured as the distance in the number of seats, as a proportion of the total seats (i.e., districted seats and at-large seats), that the minority is from proportional representation, based on total minority population. Total minority population is used rather than minority voting-age population because proportional representation is often popularly perceived, as well as couched by elected officials, as relative to overall population. The behavior of a district-elected minority to defend a proposed minority-opportunity district is dependent upon the common conceptualization of what constitutes proportional representation.

In most cases, the minority will be underrepresented by any number of seats in addition to a fraction of a seat. The interval-level data require that a fraction of a seat either be rounded up or rounded down to the next whole seat. The group that is underrepresented by the largest fraction (i.e., the plurality) has the greatest claim to the whole seat. The rounding of fractions in this manner fits well theoretically. Given a city with just two groups, either black and Anglo or Hispanic and Anglo, the minority group's movement toward proportional representation is necessarily at the "expense" of the representation of the remaining group. In this zero-sum context, a normative argument is made that there is a qualitative difference between the minority group being underrepresented, say, by one-third of a seat or by two-thirds of a seat. In the former the minority's acquisition of a whole seat will place it two-thirds of a seat above proportional representation, moving the minority further from absolute proportional representation while eroding white representation from one-third above proportional representation to two-thirds below. But in the latter, the minority's acquisition of a whole seat will move both the minority group and the white group closer to absolute proportional representation. Therefore, the situation in which the minority is underrepresented by two-thirds of a seat has a greater normative claim to an additional seat than the situation in which the minority is underrepresented by one-third of a seat. The same plurality rule will apply when there are three or more groups.

DIVESTED MINORITY INCUMBENT ADVOCACY

Divested minority incumbent advocacy is operationalized as the proportion of the total council (i.e., districted seats and at-large seats) that a minority elected at-large constitutes at the time of redistricting. The lower end of the theoretical range is 0 while the higher end may never quite equal 1. A council either without at-large seats or with at-large seats, but no minorities elected at-large, will necessarily have a score of 0. The presence of a minority elected at-large increases the score above 0. Since a city must necessarily have at minimum two districted seats to be included in the study, the proportion of a city's council that is at-large will never equal 1.

PRECLEARANCE

Cities subject to section 5 preclearance under the Voting Rights Act are measured as a dichotomous variable, 1 indicating coverage and 0 indicating noncoverage. Section 4(b) contains the conditions for coverage under the racial provisions, and section 4(f) contains the conditions for coverage under the language minority provisions. Coverage by section 4(b) is used as an explanation for the presence of black minority-opportunity districts, while coverage by section 4(f) is used as an explanation for the presence of Hispanic minority-opportunity districts. Covered jurisdictions are listed in the Code of Federal Regulations Title 28, volume 2, parts 51 and 55.

COURT INTERVENTION

Court intervention occurred when section 2 litigation over councilmanic districts was lost by the city, or settled, in the decade prior to the 1990 round of redistricting. Court intervention is operationalized as a dichotomous variable, 1 indicating intervention and 0 indicating nonintervention. These data are gathered from telephone, fax, and mail surveys of the cities' legal departments.

MINORITY PRESENCE ON GOVERNING BODY

The assumption behind measuring 'minority presence on governing body' is that minority elected officials are usually the preferred representatives of their respective groups. Minorities, for example, have consistently demonstrated their preferences for minority representatives through their voting behavior (Vanderleeuw 1990; Murray and Vedlitz 1978; Reeves 1997, esp. 76–90; Carsey 1995; Lieske and Hillard 1984; Sigleman et al. 1995). These representatives also may better represent the preferences of their respective groups. The assumption that minority elected officials make a difference finds its theoretical roots in the fact that a minority's descriptive representative is drawn from a group that collectively shares a unique historical experience and, therefore, will likely incorporate these preferences into positions on public policy issues (Karnig and Welch 1980, 13, 108–41). See chapter 2 for a more detailed discussion of minority descriptive representation.

The simple task of "head counting" can be used as an empirical measure of the presence of minorities on a city council, although it is often criticized as a crude measure of representation. Minority presence on a governing body is best measured as the *proportion* of all districted council members that are either Hispanic or black elected from respective Hispanic or black minority-opportunity districts. This proportion is identified for each city for the first, second, and third elections following the 1990 round of redistricting. Since the adoption dates of redistricting plans and terms of office for districted council members may vary from city to city, and since a particular city may have staggered district elections, specific years are not identified as the cut points at which to measure the proportion of the districted council that is minority.

RESOURCE DISPARITY

Engstrom and McDonald (1986; 1987, 247–49) measure income disparities as the ratio of black median income to white median income taken from U.S. Census Bureau figures. The authors find that the correlation between income and education is high; therefore, they use income alone because it has the most explanatory power of the two variables. Resource disparity in this study is the ratio of citywide either Hispanic or black median income to the median income of non-Hispanic whites. For example, the measure of black-white resource disparity is calculated as follows:

$$RD = \frac{\text{(Median Income Non-Hispanic whites — Median Income of Blacks)}}{\text{Median Income of Blacks}}$$

A resource disparity score of 0 indicates no difference between the median incomes of the two groups, while a resource disparity score of 1 indicates that the non-Hispanic white median income is twice (200 percent) that of the specified minority.

PARTISAN ELECTIONS

The operationalization of partisan elections is a dichotomous variable, 1 indicating partisan elections and 0 indicating absence of partisan elections. An election is identified as partisan if at least a single party's name or symbol appears on the government-printed election ballot in association with a candidate.

DISTRICT POPULATION DENSITY

District population density is a measure of the physical density of the population per square mile within the minority-opportunity district weighted for the over-all population size of the city. That is, district population density is the voting-age population per square mile of minority-opportunity district as a percent of the citywide population. If more than one either Hispanic or black minority-opportunity district is present, then the mean of the district population densities is used.

Chapter 4 has made complete our model by specifying specific empirical measures of the variables and has set the stage for testing the hypothesized relationships and reporting the findings, the focus of the next several chapters.

CHAPTER FIVE

The Adoption of Hispanic and Black Minority-Opportunity Districts: Model Testing and Findings

With the theoretical development complete and the specifics of variable measurement in hand, we are now ready to turn to testing the proposed model and presenting the findings. This chapter presents the tests of the first general hypothesis that posits the theoretical maximal proportion of minority-opportunity districts (system aptitude) as the primary explanation for the actual adoption of minority-opportunity districts. Also tested are five subhypotheses positing the conditioning effect of the five additional variables—political tenability, vested advocacy, divested advocacy, preclearance, and court intervention—on this general relationship.

Defining what percent minority may constitute an opportunity district is much debated. As you may recall, for the purpose of this study we have decided to test the relationship at three opportunity threshold levels, 60, 55, and 50 percent either Hispanic or black voting-age population. Table 5.1 provides the number of cities examined in each analysis for each voting-age population threshold, the total number of theoretically possible Hispanic and black minority-opportunity districts, and the number of such districts actually adopted. At the 60 percent threshold there are 42 cities that have the aptitude to create at least a single Hispanic minority-opportunity district. These 42 cities provide, in sum, the possibility of creating a theoretical maximal 118 Hispanic minority-opportunity districts, but the number actually adopted is only 24. At the 55 percent threshold, the number of cities that have the aptitude to create at least a single Hispanic minority-opportunity district increases by 1 to 43. The lower threshold increases the theoretical maximal number of Hispanic minority-opportunity districts by 14 (to 132), and the number of such districts actually adopted by 8 (to 32). The lowering of the threshold to 50 percent again adds another city, increases the number of theoretical districts by another 12 (to 144), and increases the number of districts actually adopted by another 16 (to 48). As the threshold decreases, the average number of theoretical Hispanic districts per city increases from 2.81 to 3.07 to 3.27. And, in similar fashion, as the threshold decreases, the average number of Hispanic districts actually adopted per city increases from .57 to .74 to 1.09.

There are 83 cities that have the aptitude to create at least a single black minority-opportunity district at the 60 percent threshold. These 83 cities have the ability to yield a theoretical maximal 290 black minority-opportunity districts. Within these cities, 143 black minority-opportunity districts actually are adopted. At the 55 percent threshold, the number of cities that have the aptitude to create at least a single black minority-opportunity district increases by 1 to 84. The lower threshold increases the theoretical maximal number of black minority-opportunity districts by 32 (to 322), and the number of actual districts adopted by 16 (to 159). Lowering the threshold to 50 percent adds 2 cities, increases the number of theoretical districts by 36 (to 358), and increases the number of actual districts by 22 (to 181). The average number of theoretical black districts per city increases from 3.49 to 3.83 to 4.16 as the threshold decreases. The average number of black districts adopted per city increases from 1.72 to 1.89 to 2.10 as the threshold decreases.

TABLE 5.1

NUMBER OF CITIES EXAMINED, THEORETICAL MAXIMAL NUMBER OF DISTRICTS, AND ACTUAL NUMBER OF DISTRICTS ADOPTED BY MINORITY STATUS AND BY VOTING-AGE POPULATION THRESHOLD

	60% VAP MIN.-OPP. THRESHOLD	55% VAP MIN.-OPP. THRESHOLD	50% VAP MIN.-OPP. THRESHOLD
Hispanic			
Cities (N)	42	43	44
Theoretical Districts (N)	118 [2.81]	132 [3.07]	144 [3.27]
Actual Districts Adopted (N)	24 [0.57]	32 [0.74]	48 [1.09]
Black			
Cities (N)	83	84	86
Theoretical Districts (N)	290 [3.49]	322 [3.83]	358 [4.16]
Actual Districts Adopted (N)	143 [1.72]	159 [1.89]	181[2.10]

Note: Numbers in brackets are means.

Table 5.2 provides descriptive statistics for the variables Hispanic system aptitude (HSA), Hispanic-opportunity districts (HOD), black system aptitude (BSA), and black-opportunity districts (BOD) on the metric to be used in the regression equations. The Hispanic and black system aptitude variables are the *proportion* of a city's total districts that can be theoretically either Hispanic or black minority-opportunity, respectively. For example, on average, .358 of all districts within each city may be theoretically 60 percent Hispanic in voting-age population. The average proportion of each city's districts that may be theoretically Hispanic minority-opportunity districts increases from .358 to .387 to .409 as the threshold decreases. In two cities (Miami and El Paso) within the universe of Hispanic cities at each threshold level, the proportion of the city's districts that may be theoretically Hispanic minority-opportunity is equal to the total number of districts (i.e., the maximum proportion is equal to 1). The minimum proportion that may be Hispanic minority-opportunity districts at each of the three thresholds is found to be .047 (Cleveland). The standard deviation about the mean proportion is .225 at the 60 percent threshold, .245 at the 55 percent threshold, and .261 at the 50 percent threshold. This suggests both that there is a considerable amount of variation in the system aptitude for Hispanic cities and that this variation increases as the threshold decreases.

Likewise, the Hispanic and black minority-opportunity district variables are the *proportion* of a city's total districts that are actually adopted as Hispanic or black minority-opportunity, respectively. For example, on average, .078 of all districts within each city are Hispanic minority-opportunity at the 60 percent threshold. The average proportion of each city's districts that are actually Hispanic minority-opportunity increases from .078 to .104 to .145 as the threshold decreases. In one city (Miami) within the universe of cities at each threshold level, the proportion of districts that has been adopted as Hispanic minority-opportunity is .800. There are several cities at each threshold that have no districts adopted as Hispanic minority-opportunity (i.e., the minimum proportion is equal to 0). The standard deviation about the mean proportion is .189 at the 60 percent threshold, .203 at the 55 percent threshold, and .205 at the 50 percent threshold.

Table 5.2 reveals both the similarities between the system aptitudes for Hispanic and black cities and an emerging contrast between the actual adoption of Hispanic and black districts. First, note that the Hispanic system aptitude is quite similar to the black system aptitude. For example, at the 60 percent threshold, the mean Hispanic system aptitude is .358, and the standard deviation is .225, while for black system aptitude the mean is .377, and the standard deviation is .238. These similarities hold across the other thresholds. System aptitude, recall, is simply a function of the number of total districts within a city relative to the sizes of the particular minority and remaining populations. The concept of 'system aptitude' has been developed to account for the mechanical parameters faced by redistricters independent of the more political aspects of redistricting. The similarities between Hispanic and black system aptitudes suggest that, as far as the mathematical ability to create minority-opportunity districts is concerned, the universe of cities in the Hispanic analysis is quite similar to those in the black analysis. It is an important point to observe these initial similarities in the status of Hispanic and black cities under analysis because, as this chapter and the next will illustrate, the forces at work in the districting process play-out in markedly different ways for the adoption of Hispanic-opportunity districts relative black-opportunity districts.

Along this vein, note the proportion of Hispanic minority-opportunity districts that have been adopted relative to the proportion of black minority-opportunity districts that have been adopted. For example, within the Hispanic cities, on average, only .078 of a city's districts actually were adopted as minority-opportunity at the 60 percent threshold, while within the black cities the proportion, on average, was nearly 2.5 times that number, .190. At the 55 and 50 percent thresholds, proportionately the shares of adopted black minority-opportunity districts are, respectively, double and 1.5 times the number of adopted Hispanic minority-opportunity districts. This, on its face, suggests that, all else equal, black opportunity districts are more likely to be adopted relative to Hispanic opportunity districts, and this disparity becomes increasingly acute as the VAP threshold increases. However, the theory presented above suggests that all else is not equal—there may be other conditions at work in the Hispanic cities under analysis that are not present in the black cities under analysis, and vice versa. The design of this chapter is an empirical investigation of these other factors that may condition the translation from system aptitude to actual adoption of minority-opportunity districts, a task that we now address.

Regression equations provide the basis for testing both the first general relationship and the hypothesized conditional relationships for Hispanic and black cities. The first general relationship asserts the theoretical maximal proportion of a city's districts that may be minority-opportunity as the primary explanation for the proportion of a city's districts that have actually been adopted as minority-opportunity. The dependent variables, the presence of adopted Hispanic and black minority-opportunity districts, are specified as HOD and BOD, respectively. The independent variables, the theoretical potential Hispanic and black-opportunity districts (i.e., Hispanic and black system aptitude), are specified as HSA and BSA, respectively.

$$HOD = a + b1HSA$$
$$BOD = a + b1BSA$$

a is the intercept
b is the slope coefficient

TABLE 5.2

PROPORTION OF A CITY'S DISTRICTS THAT MAY BE THEORETICALLY MINORITY-OPPORTUNITY AND PROPORTION OF A CITY'S DISTRICTS THAT ARE ACTUALLY MINORITY-OPPORTUNITY BY MINORITY STATUS AND VOTING-AGE POPULATION THRESHOLD

	60% VAP MIN.-OPP. THRESHOLD	55% VAP MIN.-OPP. THRESHOLD	50% VAP MIN.-OPP. THRESHOLD
Hispanic System Aptitude (HSA):			
Mean	.358	.387	.409
Maximum	1	1	1
Minimum	.047	.047	.047
Std. Deviation	.225	.245	.261
Hispanic Opportunity Districts (HOD):			
Mean	.078	.104	.145
Maximum	.800	.800	.800
Minimum	0	0	0
Std. Deviation	.189	.203	.205
Black System Aptitude (BSA):			
Mean	.377	.417	.456
Maximum	1	1	1
Minimum	.050	.050	.050
Std. Deviation	.238	.275	.280
Black Opportunity Districts (BOD):			
Mean	.190	.211	.231
Maximum	.875	.875	.875
Minimum	0	0	0
Std. Deviation	.206	.215	.226

The predicted value of the dependent variable (the proportion of a city's districts that have been adopted as either Hispanic or black minority-opportunity) is dependent upon the intercept as well as the slope coefficient. Assuming an intercept (a) of near or equal to 0, an unstandardized regression coefficient, or slope coefficient (b), approaching 1.0 means that the theoretical maximal proportion of districts that can be minority-opportunity tends to be about the same as the proportion of actual adopted minority-opportunity districts. While the proportion of actual minority-opportunity districts may not exceed the theoretical maximal proportion of minority-opportunity districts, a slope coefficient may exceed 1 when the intercept is negative (for more detailed explication of regression techniques, see Blalock 1979, Cohen and Cohen 1983).

The relationships between the system aptitude and the proportion of adopted minority-opportunity districts across the three thresholds of 60, 55, and 50 percent voting-age population are reported in table 5.3. The slope coefficient for 60 percent Hispanic voting-age population is .702, for 55 percent .657, and for 50 percent .704. These coefficients have a range of no more that 4.7 points between any two suggesting that the slope of the regression line is fairly similar across the three thresholds. The slope coefficient for 60 percent black voting-age population is .785, for 55 percent .710, and for 50 percent .741. These coefficients have a range of no more than 7.5 points between any two, once again suggesting similarity across the thresholds.

Note the relative differences between the Hispanic coefficients and the black coefficients at each threshold. In each case the black coefficient is larger than the Hispanic coefficient. At the 60 percent threshold the difference is 8.3 points, at the 55 percent threshold 5.3 points, and at the 50 percent threshold 3.7 points. Likewise, the R^2 coefficient, providing a measure of how much of the variance in the dependent variable is accounted for by the independent variable, is larger for blacks relative to Hispanics at each threshold. This suggests that the system aptitude for blacks accounts for the presence of black minority-opportunity districts better than does the system aptitude for Hispanics accounts for the presence of Hispanic minority-opportunity districts.

Notice also that the intercept—the location where the regression line crosses the vertical *Y*-axis—is below 0 for each equation. For Hispanic cities, the intercepts vary from -.174 to -.143 and for black cities from -.106 to -.084, depending on the threshold. The location of the intercepts is explained by the fact that there are no cities in the study with a system aptitude, measured as a proportion, of 0.0. Recall that by definition a city must have the aptitude to create at least a single theoretical minority-opportunity district to be included in the study (i.e., proportion must be greater than 0.0). Since many of the cities in the study have a small number of council districts—five or seven—this means that the minimum system aptitude measure may begin at .200 (for a five-district council) or .143 (for a seven-district council). In the universe of either Hispanic or black cities, there are a number with a system aptitude to create just one or two minority-opportunity districts. Further, a number of these cities having such an aptitude have not adopted a proportional share of actual districts. That is, some cities with a system aptitude of .20 may actually have a proportion of adopted minority-opportunity districts that is 0.0, cities with an aptitude of .40 may actually have a proportion of adopted minority-opportunity districts that is .20, and so forth. The regression line fitting the data may intercept the horizontal *X*-axis well to the right of 0.0. Thus, the *Y*-intercept will likely not be at or near 0 but, rather, within the stated range. Provided the above slope coefficients, the larger negative *Y*-intercepts for Hispanic cities relative to black cities suggests that the Hispanic regression lines intercept the *X*-axis to the right of the regression lines for black cities.

TABLE 5.3

REGRESSION COEFFICIENT ESTIMATES FOR THE RELATIONSHIP BETWEEN SYSTEM APTITUDE AND THE PRESENCE OF MINORITY-OPPORTUNITY DISTRICTS BY MINORITY STATUS AND VOTING-AGE POPULATION THRESHOLD

	60% VAP MIN.-OPP. THRESHOLD	55% VAP MIN.-OPP. THRESHOLD	50% VAP MIN.-OPP. THRESHOLD
Hispanic			
Intercept	-.174 (.030)	-.150 (.036)	-.143 (.026)
Slope Coefficient	.702 (.072)	.657 (.078)	.704 (.054)
R^2	.698	.622	.798
S.E.E.	.103	.124	.092
Cities (N)	42	43	44
Black			
Intercept	-.105 (.019)	-.084 (.018)	-.106 (.019)
Slope Coefficient	.785 (.042)	.710 (.036)	.741 (.035)
R2	.815	.829	.839
S.E.E.	.089	.089	.091
Cities (N)	83	84	86

Notes: All slope coefficients are significant at the .001 level.
Numbers in parentheses are standard errors for the coefficients.

The aptitude of a system alone may not provide a full explanation for the proportion of actual adopted minority-opportunity districts. The R^2s for Hispanics leave as much as 37.8 percent of the variance unexplained and for blacks as much as 18.5 percent unexplained. The design of this study establishes a theoretical maximal proportion of a city's districts that may be minority-opportunity and then asks what factors may account for erosion from this theoretical maximal proportion to the actual adopted proportion. The theory suggests that additional variables should be introduced as specifying variables (i.e., modifying the intercept and slope coefficient) rather than introduced as separate and distinct independent variables that have a direct, uniform impact on minority-opportunity districts across cities.[1] These five specifying variables are as follows:

PT = Political Tenability
VA = Vested Advocacy
DA = Divested Advocacy
PC = Preclearance
CI = Court Intervention

Each of these specifying variable is included in a regression to measure the conditioning effect of each on the intercept and slope coefficient.

POLITICAL TENABILITY CONDITIONING THE FIRST GENERAL RELATIONSHIP

Table 5.4 models the impact of political tenability as a specifying variable conditioning the relationship between system aptitude and the proportion of districts adopted as minority-opportunity for both Hispanics and blacks. Equations 1 through 3 present the findings at the 60 percent, 55 percent, and 50 percent Hispanic voting-age population thresholds. Equations 4 through 6 present the findings at the 60 percent, 55 percent, and 50 percent black voting-age population thresholds.

The measure of political tenability (i.e., residential segregation) has a theoretical range of 0 (indicating complete integration) to 1 (indicating complete segregation), but the "real-world" or empirical range for political tenability is smaller. For example, within the universe of cities with an aptitude to construct at least a single Hispanic minority-opportunity district at the 60 percent voting-age threshold is found an empirical range of political tenability scores that extends from a minimum of .182 (Moreno Valley, Calif.) to a maximum of .839 (Corpus Christi, Tex.). But noting just the minimum and maximum levels of segregation provides quite limited information on the nature of segregation within a set of cities. The mean level of segregation and the standard deviation above and below this mean provide a more complete picture. For example, within this same universe of cities, the average segregation score is .513, while one standard deviation below the mean is .392 and one standard deviation above the mean is .634. The dispersion of segregation scores about the mean suggests a considerable amount of variation in segregation for both Hispanic and black cities and, interestingly, the range between one standard deviation above and below the mean is nearly identical for Hispanic and black cities alike. Note also that, consistent with our theoretical expectations, the average level of segregation is lower for Hispanics relative to blacks. The average segregation score for Hispanics across the three thresholds is about .51 while the average for blacks across the three thresholds is about .69, markedly higher.[2]

The effect of introducing political tenability as an interaction term conditioning the first general relationship is the modification, or adjustment, of the slope coefficient and intercept. The coefficient for the political tenability variable, reported in the top half of table 5.4, adjusts the intercept, while the coefficient for the interaction term, also reported in the top half of table 5.4, serves as an adjustment in the slope coefficient. Reported in the bottom half of table 5.4 are the adjustments in the intercepts and slope coefficients for three different values of political tenability, specifically the mean and one standard deviation above and below the mean, when system aptitude is set at its average for that group of cities. Using equation 1 as an example, which concerns Hispanic minority-opportunity districts at the 60 percent threshold, a political tenability score of .392 (one standard deviation below the mean PT score) will result in an adjusted slope coefficient of .064 and intercept of -.105, a political tenability score of .634 (one standard deviation above the mean PT score) will produce an adjusted slope coefficient of .190 and intercept of -.188, and a political tenability score of .513 (the mean PT value) will produce an adjusted slope coefficient of .127 and intercept of -.147.

The findings show that as the value of political tenability increases from one standard deviation below to one standard deviation above the mean, so do the adjusted slope coefficients. This holds true for both Hispanic and black minority-opportunity districts at all thresholds. This means that when segregation is relatively low (i.e., at or near one standard deviation below its mean), it impacts adversely on the translation between the maximal proportion of theoretical minority-opportunity districts and the proportion of districts actually adopted. When it is relatively high (i.e., at or near one standard deviation above its mean), it impacts more positively on that translation. For example, the translation between the aptitude of a system to create 60 percent Hispanic minority-opportunity districts and the actual adoption of 60 percent Hispanic minority-opportunity districts, measured by the slope coefficient, changes relative to the level of segregation present. When the value of the political tenability score is one standard deviation below the mean, the slope coefficient is .064, meaning that a one-unit increase in the proportion of all districts that may be theoretically Hispanic minority-opportunity (i.e., system aptitude) corresponds with a 6.4 percentage point increase in one-unit of the proportion of Hispanic minority-opportunity districts actually adopted. When the value of the political tenability score is one standard deviation above the mean, the slope coefficient is .190, meaning that a one-unit increase in the proportion of all districts that may be theoretically Hispanic minority-opportunity results in a 19.0 percentage point increase in one-unit of the proportion of Hispanic minority-opportunity districts actually adopted.

Notice also that the range between the reported minimum and maximum adjusted coefficients decreases as the threshold decreases. For 60 percent Hispanic districts, the range is .126, for 55 percent .063, and for 50 percent .058. The difference between the 50 and 55 percent thresholds is modest, but the difference between the 55 and 60 percent threshold is marked. Likewise, the range for 60 percent black districts is .076, for 55 percent .025, and for 50 percent .023. Once again, the difference between the 50 and 55 percent thresholds is modest, but the difference between the 55 and 60 percent thresholds is marked.

For both Hispanics and blacks the interaction term at the 60 percent threshold is statistically significant, while the interaction terms at the 55 and 50 percent thresholds are not statistically significant. Note also that the system aptitude variable itself is not statistically significant for Hispanics at any threshold, but it is statistically significant for blacks at the 55 and 50 percent thresholds. At this point a caveat is in order. Statistical significance is an important tool when analyzing a sample. When working with samples, an important question is always, "How much confidence do we have that the

Table 5.4

Regression Coefficient Estimates of the Specifying Variable Political Tenability on the First General Relationship

	HOD = a + b1SA + b2PT + b3(SA*PT)			BOD = a + b1SA + b2PT + b3(SA*PT)		
	EQUATION 1 60% VAP	EQUATION 2 55% VAP	EQUATION 3 50% VAP	EQUATION 4 60% VAP	EQUATION 5 55% VAP	EQUATION 6 50% VAP
Intercept	.030 (.137)	-.076 (.168)	-.142 (.122)	-.112 (.146)	-.189 (.165)	-.228 (.168)
System Aptitude	-.141 (.342)	.265 (.361)	.369 (.246)	.122 (.253)	.481** (.213)	.541** (.210)
Political Tenability	-.345 (.252)	-.113 (.311)	.028 (.230)	.045 (.135)	.180 (.134)	.215 (.138)
SA * PT Interaction	1.458* (.529)	.671 (.627)	.527 (.439)	.834** (.347)	.258 (.295)	.206 (.297)
N	42	43	44	83	84	86
Adjusted R^2	.739	.624	.826	.845	.843	.853
Std. Error of Est.	.096	.124	.085	.081	.085	.086

Notes: Numbers in parentheses are standard errors for the unstandardized regression coefficients.
* = Significance at .05 level, ** = Significance at .01 level, *** = Significance at .001 level

REGRESSION COEFFICIENT ESTIMATES OF THE SPECIFYING VARIABLE
POLITICAL TENABILITY ON THE FIRST GENERAL RELATIONSHIP *(CONTINUED)*

	HOD = a + b1SA + b2PT + b3(SA*PT)			BOD = a + b1SA + b2PT + b3(SA*PT)		
	EQUATION 1 60% VAP	EQUATION 2 55% VAP	EQUATION 3 50% VAP	EQUATION 4 60% VAP	EQUATION 5 55% VAP	EQUATION 6 50% VAP
System Aptitude:						
Mean	.358	.387	.409	.377	.417	.456
PT Range:						
1-Std. Dev. Below	.392	.392	.386	.566	.567	.562
Mean	.513	.512	.507	.685	.686	.682
1-Std. Dev. Above	.634	.632	.629	.805	.804	.802
Adjustment:						
For 1-Std. Dev. Below Mean PT:						
Slope Coeff.	.064	.366	.458	.299	.542	.593
Intercept	-.105	-.120	-.131	-.087	-.087	-.107
For Mean PT:						
Slope Coeff.	.127	.387	.488	.337	.554	.605
Intercept	-.147	-.134	-.128	-.081	-.066	-.082
For 1-Std. Dev. Above Mean PT:	.126					
Slope Coeff.	.190	.429	.516	.375	.567	.616
Intercept	-.188	-.147	-.124	-.076	-.047	-.056

findings derived from our sample may be inferred to the larger universe?" In this study we have not taken a sample of cities from a larger universe of cities. Rather, we have acquired data for the entire universe of U.S. cities that meet our selection criteria. Thus, it may be argued, that the importance of reporting statistical significance is limited and contributes little to the substantive interpretation of data. However, due to convention, we report significance levels in each analysis.

The substantive interpretation of these numbers is that the minority voting-age population threshold conditions, as expected, the importance of segregation in the translation between system aptitude and the actual adoption of minority-opportunity districts. When 60 percent minority-opportunity districts are sought, the impact of the level of minority segregation is more demonstrative relative to when 55 percent minority-opportunity districts are sought. However, the impact of segregation between the 55 and 50 percent thresholds is much more modest, especially for blacks.

Finally, a comparison of the R^2s presented in table 5.3 with that of table 5.4 may indicate the contribution to the amount of explained variance in the dependent variable derived from the modeling of political tenability as an interaction.[3] For Hispanics the R^2 increases from .698 to an adjusted R^2 of .739 for the 60 percent threshold, .622 to .624 for the 55 percent threshold, and .798 to .826 for the 50 percent threshold. For black cities the amount of variance in the dependent variable explained by the addition of political tenability increases from an R^2 of .815 to an adjusted R^2 of .845 for the 60 percent threshold, .829 to .843 for the 55 percent threshold, and .839 to .853 for the 50 percent threshold. For both Hispanic and black cities the largest contribution is found at the 60 percent threshold.

MINORITY INCUMBENT ADVOCACY CONDITIONING THE FIRST GENERAL RELATIONSHIP

Table 5.5 models the impact of vested minority incumbent advocacy as a specifying variable conditioning the relationship between system aptitude and the proportion of districts adopted as minority-opportunity for both Hispanics and blacks. Equations 1 through 3 present the findings at the 60, 55, and 50 percent Hispanic voting-age population thresholds, while equations 4 through 6 present the findings at the 60, 55, and 50 percent black voting-age population thresholds.

Vested minority incumbent advocacy addresses either the absence or the presence of a minority incumbent in conjunction with minority underrepresentation. The measure of vested minority incumbent advocacy has a theoretical range from 0, indicating the absence of either a Hispanic or black incumbent or incumbents in a districted council seat(s) at the time of redistricting and increases toward 1, indicating the presence of either a Hispanic or black incumbent or incumbents in conjunction with the underrepresentation of said minority at the time of redistricting (a more detailed explanation of this measure is found in chapter 4). The empirical range, of course, is truncated within this larger theoretical range. Reported are the impacts of three levels of vested minority incumbent advocacy (the mean, one standard deviation above this mean, and one standard deviation below it) on the relationship between system aptitude and the presence of minority-opportunity districts when system aptitude is set at its average for a set of cities. For example, at the 60 percent threshold for Hispanics the mean level of vested Hispanic incumbent advocacy produces an adjusted slope coefficient of .467 and intercept of -.158, meaning that a one-unit increase in the proportion of all districts that may be theoretically Hispanic minority-opportunity (i.e., system aptitude) results in a 46.7 percentage point increase in one-unit of the proportion of Hispanic minority-opportunity districts actually adopted. When vested Hispanic advocacy is one standard deviation below its mean, the adjusted slope coefficient is .418 and intercept is -.088. When vested Hispanic advocacy is one standard deviation above its mean, the adjusted slope coefficient is .547 and intercept is -.275.[4]

The findings show that both the system aptitude and interaction variables for Hispanic cities are statistically significant at each of the three thresholds. The findings also show that as the values for vested Hispanic incumbent advocacy increase from one standard deviation below to one standard deviation above the mean, so do the adjusted slope coefficients for system aptitude. This means that when vested Hispanic incumbent advocacy is relatively low (i.e., at or near one standard deviation below its mean), it does not increase the translation between the proportion of theoretical minority-opportunity districts and the proportion of districts actually adopted. In fact, the adjusted slope coefficient and intercept for one standard deviation below the mean is identical to the slope coefficient and intercept in the top half of the table. There is no adjustment to the slope coefficient or intercept due to the fact that the reported minimums for VA are 0. When vested Hispanic incumbent advocacy is relatively high (i.e., at or near one standard deviation above its mean), it impacts positively on that translation. The range between the value of the adjusted slope at the minimum value to VA and at a VA score of one standard deviation above the mean for cities at the 60 percent Hispanic threshold is .129, at the 55 percent threshold .101, and at the 50 percent threshold .100. Clearly vested advocacy conditions the relationship at each threshold. Substantively, this means that districted Hispanic incumbency combined with Hispanic underrepresentation at the time of redistricting impacts positively the adoption of Hispanic minority-opportunity districts at each threshold.

The findings show that the system aptitude variable is statistically significant at each of the three thresholds for black cities, and the interaction variable does not reach significance. The findings also show that the ranges between the adjusted slope coefficients at the reported minimum and at one standard deviation above the mean for VA are fairly small, and the ranges change relatively little between thresholds for black minority-opportunity districts, in contrast to

TABLE 5.5

REGRESSION COEFFICIENT ESTIMATES OF THE SPECIFYING VARIABLE VESTED ADVOCACY ON THE FIRST GENERAL RELATIONSHIP

	HOD = a + b1SA + b2VA + b3(SA*VA)			BOD = a + b1SA + b2VA + b3(SA*VA)		
	EQUATION 1 60% VAP	EQUATION 2 55% VAP	EQUATION 3 50% VAP	EQUATION 4 60% VAP	EQUATION 5 55% VAP	EQUATION 6 50% VAP
Intercept	-.088 (.031)	-.049 (.027)	-.080 (.024)	-.100 (.026)	-.091 (.023)	-.021 (.017)
System Aptitude	.418*** (.100)	.229*** (.076)	.454*** (.063)	.746*** (.045)	.710*** (.039)	.460*** (.032)
Vested Aptitude	-4.157** (1.455)	-.069 (1.489)	-.595 (1.430)	-.379 (1.096)	1.186 (.957)	.592 (.899)
SA * VA Interaction	7.985*** (1.749)	5.960*** (1.764)	4.224** (1.658)	.860 (1.409)	-1.185 (1.040)	-.493 (.942)
N	42	43	44	83	84	86
Adjusted R^2	.806	.841	.877	.812	.826	.712
Std. Error of Est.	.083	.080	.072	.089	.089	.068

Notes: Numbers in parentheses are standard errors for the unstandardized regression coefficients.
* = Significance at .05 level, ** = Significance at .01 level, *** = Significance at .001 level

REGRESSION COEFFICIENT ESTIMATES OF THE SPECIFYING VARIABLE
VESTED ADVOCACY ON THE FIRST GENERAL RELATIONSHIP *(CONTINUED)*

	HOD = a + b1SA + b2VA + b3(SA*VA)			BOD = a + b1SA + b2VA + b3(SA*VA)		
	EQUATION 1 60% VAP	EQUATION 2 55% VAP	EQUATION 3 50% VAP	EQUATION 4 60% VAP	EQUATION 5 55% VAP	EQUATION 6 50% VAP
System Aptitude:						
Mean	.358	.387	.409	.377	.417	.456
VA Range:						
1-Std. Dev. Below ◆	.000	.000	.000	.000	.000	.000
Mean	.017	.017	.016	.016	.016	.016
1-Std. Dev. Above	.045	.044	.060	.058	.058	.058
Adjustment: For 1-Std. Dev. Below Mean VA:						
Slope Coeff.	.418	.229	.458	.746	.710	.460
Intercept	-.088	-.049	-.080	-.100	-.091	-.021
For Mean VA:						
Slope Coeff.	.467	.268	.482	.751	.702	.456
Intercept	-.158	-.050	-.089	-.106	-.072	-.011
For 1-Std. Dev. Above Mean VA:		.129				
Slope Coeff.	.547	.330	.558	.764	.681	.446
Intercept	-.275	-.052	-.115	-.121	-.022	.013

◆ For the VA Range, one standard deviation below the mean has been truncated to the real-world minimum of .000.

Hispanic cities. At the black 60 percent threshold, the range is .018, at the 55 percent threshold .029, and at the 50 percent threshold .014. This means that at the 60 percent threshold districted black incumbency combined with black underrepresentation impacts only slightly in a positive direction the translation between the proportion of districts that could be, theoretically, black minority-opportunity districts and the proportion of districts that are actually black minority-opportunity districts. Notice, however, that vested black incumbent advocacy impacts the relationship in a negative direction at the 55 and 50 percent thresholds, although again only slightly. It must be kept in mind that ranges at the 60, 55, and 50 percent thresholds are quite small indicating that the impact of vested black incumbent advocacy, whether positive or negative, is only slight. Vested black incumbent advocacy has little impact, while vested Hispanic incumbent advocacy has marked impact, in conditioning the hypothesized general relationship.

Finally, a comparison of the R^2s between table 5.3 and table 5.5 may indicate the contribution to the amount of explained variance in the dependent variable derived from the modeling of vested minority incumbent advocacy as an interaction term. For Hispanics, the R^2 changes from .739 to an adjusted R^2 of .806 for the 60 percent threshold, .622 to .841 for the 55 percent threshold, and .798 to .877 for the 50 percent threshold. Clearly, the variable contributes to the amount of variance explained. For black districts, however, based on the adjusted R^2s , the same or less variance in the dependent variable is explained when vested minority incumbent advocacy is added to the equation. An R^2 of .815 is changed to an adjusted R^2 of .812 for the 60 percent threshold, .829 to .826 for the 55 percent threshold, and .839 to .712 for the 50 percent threshold.

DIVESTED MINORITY INCUMBENT ADVOCACY CONDITIONING THE FIRST GENERAL RELATIONSHIP

Table 5.6 models the impact of divested minority incumbent advocacy as a specifying variable conditioning the relationship between system aptitude and the proportion of districts adopted as Hispanic and black minority-opportunity. Equations 1 through 3 present the findings at the 60, 55, and 50 percent Hispanic voting-age population thresholds, while equations 4 through 6 present the findings at the 60, 55, and 50 percent black voting-age population thresholds.

Divested minority incumbent advocacy addresses either the absence or the presence at the time of redistricting of either a Hispanic or a black minority council member or members elected at-large. The measure of divested minority incumbent advocacy has a theoretical range from 0, indicating the absence of either a Hispanic or black incumbent in an at-large council seat at the time of redistricting, and increases toward 1, indicating at the time of redistricting the presence of at least a single said minority elected at-large, measured as the proportion of the total council (a more detailed explanation of this measure is found in chapter 4). The empirical range is truncated within this larger theoretical range. Reported are the impacts of three levels of divested minority incumbent advocacy (the mean, one standard deviation above this mean, and one standard deviation below it) on the relationship between system aptitude and the presence of minority-opportunity districts when system aptitude is set at its average for a set of cities. For example, at the 60 percent Hispanic threshold the mean level of divested Hispanic incumbent advocacy produces an adjusted slope coefficient of .704 and intercept of -.166, meaning that a one-unit increase in the proportion of all districts that may be theoretically Hispanic minority-opportunity (i.e., system aptitude) results in a 70.4 percentage point increase in one-unit of the proportion of Hispanic minority-opportunity districts actually adopted. When divested Hispanic advocacy is 1 standard deviation below its mean, the adjusted slope coefficient is .714 and intercept is -.172. When divested Hispanic advocacy is one standard deviation above its mean, the adjusted slope coefficient is .660 and intercept is -.140.

The findings show that the system aptitude variable is statistically significant for Hispanic cities, and the interaction term is not statistically significant at each of the three thresholds. The findings also show that as the values for divested Hispanic incumbent advocacy increase from 1 standard deviation below to 1 standard deviation above the mean for Hispanic cities, the adjusted slope coefficients decrease. This holds true for all thresholds. When divested Hispanic incumbent advocacy is relatively low (i.e., at 1 standard deviation below its mean), it does not increase the translation between the proportion of all districts that may be theoretically minority-opportunity districts and the proportion of all districts that are actually adopted as minority-opportunity. The adjusted slope coefficient and intercept for one standard deviation below the mean are identical to the slope coefficient and intercept in the top half of the table. There is no adjustment to the slope coefficient or intercept due to the fact that the minimums for DA are 0. When divested Hispanic incumbent advocacy is relatively high (i.e., at one standard deviation above its mean), it impacts adversely the translation. This means, contrary to our hypothesis, that the presence of an at-large Hispanic council member at the time of redistricting may decrease the likelihood that Hispanic minority-opportunity districts will be adopted. The range between the minimum and maximum slope coefficients reported in the lower portion of table 5.6 for the cities at the 60 percent Hispanic threshold is .054, at the 55 percent threshold is .015, and at the 50 percent threshold is .038. The ranges between these reported minimum and maximum slope coefficients are quite small.

The findings show that the system aptitude variable is statistically significant, and the interaction term is not statistically significant at each of the three thresholds for black cities. The findings also show that as the values for divested black incumbent advocacy increase from one standard deviation below to one

TABLE 5.6

REGRESSION COEFFICIENT ESTIMATES OF THE SPECIFYING VARIABLE DIVESTED ADVOCACY ON THE FIRST GENERAL RELATIONSHIP

	HOD = a + b1SA + b2DA + b3(SA*DA)			BOD = a + b1SA + b2DA + b3(SA*DA)		
	EQUATION 1 60% VAP	EQUATION 2 55% VAP	EQUATION 3 50% VAP	EQUATION 4 60% VAP	EQUATION 5 55% VAP	EQUATION 6 50% VAP
Intercept	-.172 (.030)	-.151 (.037)	-.145 (.026)	-.088 (.096)	-.074 (.083)	-.095 (.112)
System Aptitude	.714*** (.071)	.669*** (.081)	.719*** (.054)	.731*** (.051)	.674*** (.043)	.720*** (.041)
Divested Advocacy	1.239 (3.318)	-.142 (2.931)	.978 (3.001)	-.420 (.294)	-.212 (.288)	-.564 (.353)
SA * DA Interaction	-5.797 (7.698)	-1.524 (5.214)	-3.736 (5.131)	.833 (.450)	.498 (.153)	.757 (.445)
N	42	43	44	83	84	86
Adjusted R^2	.707	.614	.805	.817	.827	.838
Std. Error of Est.	.102	.125	.090	.088	.089	.091

Notes: Numbers in parentheses are standard errors for the unstandardized regression coefficients.
* = Significance at .05 level, ** = Significance at .01 level, *** = Significance at .001 level

REGRESSION COEFFICIENT ESTIMATES OF THE SPECIFYING VARIABLE
DIVESTED ADVOCACY ON THE FIRST GENERAL RELATIONSHIP *(CONTINUED)*

	HOD = a + b1SA + b2DA + b3(SA*DA)			BOD = a + b1SA + b2DA + b3(SA*DA)		
	EQUATION 1 60% VAP	EQUATION 2 55% VAP	EQUATION 3 50% VAP	EQUATION 4 60% VAP	EQUATION 5 55% VAP	EQUATION 6 50% VAP
System Aptitude:						
Mean	.358	.387	.409	.377	.417	.456
DA Range:						
1-Std. Dev. Below ◆	.000	.000	.000	.000	.000	.000
Mean	.005	.005	.004	.040	.039	.039
1-Std. Dev. Above	.026	.025	.025	.126	.124	.123
Adjustment:						
For 1-Std. Dev. Below Mean DA:						
Slope Coeff.	.718	.669	.719	.713	.674	.720
Intercept	-.172	-.151	-.145	-.088	-.074	-.095
For Mean DA:						
Slope Coeff.	.704	.666	.712	.743	.682	.733
Intercept	-.166	-.152	-.141	-.104	-.082	-.116
For 1-Std. Dev. Above Mean DA:	.054					
Slope Coeff.	.660	.654	.681	.770	.699	.762
Intercept	-.140	-.154	-.121	-.140	-.100	-.164

standard deviation above the mean, so too do the adjusted slope coefficients increase for black cities. This is in contrast to the Hispanic cities. This suggests a positive relationship, meaning that the presence of an at-large black council member at the time of redistricting may increase the likelihood that black minority-opportunity districts will be adopted. The range between the minimum and maximum adjusted slope coefficients is .057 at the 60 percent threshold, .025 at the 55 percent threshold, and .042 at the 50 percent threshold.

Finally, a comparison between the R^2s in table 5.3 and the adjusted R^2s in table 5.6 indicate the contribution to the amount of explained variance in the dependent variable derived from the modeling of divested minority incumbent advocacy as an interaction. For Hispanic districts, the amount of variance in the dependent variable explained by the addition of divested Hispanic incumbent advocacy is inconsequential, changing the R^2 from .698 to .707 for the 60 percent threshold, .622 to .614 for the 55 percent threshold, and .798 to .805 for the 50 percent threshold. Similarly, for black districts the amount of variance explained by the addition of divested black incumbent advocacy changes from .815 to .817 for the 60 percent threshold, .829 to .827 for the 55 percent threshold, and .839 to .838 for the 50 percent threshold.

PRECLEARANCE CONDITIONING THE FIRST GENERAL RELATIONSHIP

Table 5.7 models the impact of preclearance as a specifying variable conditioning the relationship between system aptitude and the proportion of districts adopted as minority-opportunity for both Hispanics and blacks. Equations 1 through 3 present the findings at the 60, 55, and 50 percent Hispanic voting-age population thresholds, while equations 4 through 6 present the findings at the 60, 55, and 50 percent black voting-age population thresholds.

The variable preclearance (i.e., coverage by section 4(b) of the Voting Rights Act for black opportunity districts and section 4(f) for Hispanic opportunity districts) is measured as a dichotomous variable. Therefore, preclearance has both a theoretical and empirical range of 0 to 1, 0 indicating noncoverage, and 1 indicating coverage. Table 5.7 reports how the presence of preclearance coverage conditions the general relationship when system aptitude is at its average for that group of cities.

The findings show that the system aptitude variable is statistically significant for both Hispanic and black cities, while neither the preclearance variable itself nor the interaction term are statistically significant at each of the three thresholds. The findings also show that at each voting-age population threshold for both Hispanics and blacks, the adjusted slope coefficients increase from minimum (i.e., noncoverage by preclearance) to maximum (i.e., coverage by preclearance). At first glance this means that preclearance coverage in both black and Hispanic cities impacts positively the translation from the theoretical maximal proportion of all districts that may be minority-opportunity districts to the proportion of all districts that are actually adopted as minority-opportunity districts. Note, however, the *magnitude* of the impact of preclearance on adoption. The range between the minimum and maximum adjusted slope coefficients is .048 at the 60 percent Hispanic threshold, .060 at the 55 percent threshold, and .031 at the 50 percent threshold. The ranges for black opportunity districts are also small, .018 at the 60 percent black threshold, .001 at the 55 percent threshold, and .006 at the 50 percent threshold. In relative terms, preclearance in Hispanic cities tends to increase the likelihood that minority-opportunity districts will be adopted when contrasted with preclearance in black cities. However, in both Hispanic and black cities preclearance can only be said to have changed the slope slightly.

Last, there is little or no variance in the dependent variable explained by the addition of preclearance as an interaction for both Hispanic and black districts. The R^2s remain essentially unchanged: from .698 to an adjusted R^2 of .690 for the 60 percent threshold, from .622 to .612 for the 55 percent threshold, and from .798 to .792 for the 50 percent threshold. For black districts, the amount of variance in the dependent variable explained by the addition of preclearance increases negligibly from an R^2 of .815 to an adjusted R^2 of .818 for the 60 percent threshold, .829 to .830 for the 55 percent threshold, and from .839 to .844 for the 50 percent threshold.

COURT INTERVENTION CONDITIONING THE FIRST GENERAL RELATIONSHIP

Table 5.8 models the impact of court intervention as a specifying variable conditioning the relationship between system aptitude and the proportion of districts adopted as minority-opportunity for both Hispanics and blacks. Equations 1 through 3 present the findings at the 60, 55, and 50 percent Hispanic voting-age population thresholds, while equations 4 through 6 present the findings at the 60, 55, and 50 percent black voting-age population thresholds.

The variable court intervention is dichotomous with both a theoretical and an empirical range of 0 to 1. A court intervention score of 0 indicates the absence of section 2 litigation in the decade prior to the 1990 round of redistricting, and a score of 1 indicates the occurrence of such litigation.

The findings show that both system aptitude and the interaction term are statistically significant for Hispanic cities. The findings also show that as the value of court intervention increases from 0 to 1, the slope coefficients increase as well. For Hispanic minority-opportunity districts, the range between the reported minimum and maximum adjusted coefficients is .066 at the 60 percent, .062 at the 55 percent, and .067 at the 50 percent threshold. This suggests that for Hispanic minority-opportunity districts at each threshold the occurrence of litigation in the decade preceding the 1990 round of redistricting has had a discernable impact on the general relationship.

TABLE 5.7

REGRESSION COEFFICIENT ESTIMATES OF THE SPECIFYING VARIABLE PRECLEARANCE ON THE FIRST GENERAL RELATIONSHIP

	HOD = a + b1SA + b2PC + b3(SA*PC)			BOD = a + b1SA + b2PC + b3(SA*PC)		
	EQUATION 1 60% VAP	EQUATION 2 55% VAP	EQUATION 3 50% VAP	EQUATION 4 60% VAP	EQUATION 5 55% VAP	EQUATION 6 50% VAP
Intercept	-.164 (.038)	-.130 (.044)	-.141 (.032)	-.103 (.040)	-.085 (.028)	-.106 (.031)
System Aptitude	.654*** (.094)	.595*** (.102)	.675*** (.068)	.744*** (.052)	.686*** (.045)	.707*** (.044)
Preclearance Sec. 4(f) or 4(b)	-.018 (.066)	-.054 (.080)	-.009 (.058)	.024 (.047)	.042 (.048)	.050 (.051)
SA * PC Interaction	.133 (.150)	.155 (.164)	.075 (.119)	.050 (.092)	.003 (.082)	.014 (.080)
N	42	43	44	83	84	86
Adjusted R^2	.690	.612	.792	.818	.830	.844
Std. Error of Est.	.105	.126	.093	.088	.088	.089

Notes: Numbers in parentheses are standard errors for the unstandardized regression coefficients.
* = Significance at .05 level, ** = Significance at .01 level, *** = Significance at .001 level

REGRESSION COEFFICIENT ESTIMATES OF THE SPECIFYING VARIABLE PRECLEARANCE ON THE FIRST GENERAL RELATIONSHIP *(CONTINUED)*

	HOD = a + b1SA + b2PC + b3(SA*PC)			BOD = a + b1SA + b2PC + b3(SA*PC)		
	EQUATION 1 60% VAP	EQUATION 2 55% VAP	EQUATION 3 50% VAP	EQUATION 4 60% VAP	EQUATION 5 55% VAP	EQUATION 6 50% VAP
System Aptitude:						
Mean	.358	.387	.409	.377	.417	.456
PC Range:						
Minimum PC	0	0	0	0	0	0
Maximum PC	1	1	1	1	1	1
Adjustment:						
For Minimum PC:						
Slope Coeff.	.654	.595	.675	.744	.686	.707
Intercept	-.164	-.130	-.138	-.103	-.085	-.106
For Maximum PC:	.048					
Slope Coeff.	.702	.655	.706	.762	.687	.713
Intercept	-.182	-.184	-.147	-.079	-.043	-.056

TABLE 5.8

REGRESSION COEFFICIENT ESTIMATES OF THE SPECIFYING VARIABLE COURT INTERVENTION ON THE FIRST GENERAL RELATIONSHIP

	HOD = a + b1SA + b2CI + b3(SA*CI)			BOD = a + b1SA + b2CI + b3(SA*CI)		
	EQUATION 1 60% VAP	EQUATION 2 55% VAP	EQUATION 3 50% VAP	EQUATION 4 60% VAP	EQUATION 5 55% VAP	EQUATION 6 50% VAP
Constant Intercept	-.148 (.035)	-.148 (.035)	-.131 (.030)	-.108 (.044)	-.075 (.028)	-.097 (.037)
System Aptitude	.604*** (.088)	.633*** (.104)	.653*** (.070)	.748*** (.052)	.672*** (.046)	.708*** (.040)
Court Intervention	-.046 (.059)	-.026 (.078)	-.031 (.055)	.042 (.041)	.003 (.040)	-.015 (.039)
SA * CI Interaction	.266** (.129)	.165* (.071)	.162* (.069)	-.028 (.101)	.034 (.086)	.098 (.078)
N	42	43	44	83	84	86
Adjusted R^2	.783	.685	.843	.792	.806	.858
Std. Error of Est.	.092	.119	.085	.085	.087	.080

Notes: Numbers in parentheses are standard errors for the unstandardized regression coefficients.
* = Significance at .05 level, ** = Significance at .01 level, *** = Significance at .001 level

Regression Coefficient Estimates of the Specifying Variable
Court Intervention on the First General Relationship *(continued)*

	HOD = a + b1SA + b2CI + b3(SA*CI)			BOD = a + b1SA + b2CI + b3(SA*CI)		
	EQUATION 1 60% VAP	EQUATION 2 55% VAP	EQUATION 3 50% VAP	EQUATION 4 60% VAP	EQUATION 5 55% VAP	EQUATION 6 50% VAP
System Aptitude:						
Mean	.358	.387	.409	.377	.417	.456
CI Range:						
Minimum CI	0	0	0	0	0	0
Maximum CI	1	1	1	1	1	1
Adjustment:						
For Minimum CI						
Slope Coeff.	.604	.633	.653	.748	.672	.708
Intercept	-.148	-.148	-.131	-.108	-.075	-.097
For Maximum CI						
Slope Coeff.	.670	.695	.720	.737	.686	.752
Intercept	-.194	-.174	-.162	-.066	-.072	-.112

The findings show that the variable system aptitude is statistically significant for black cities, while the interaction term is not. The findings also show that as the value of court intervention increases from 0 to 1, the adjusted slope coefficients decrease at the 60 percent threshold and increase at both the 55 and 50 percent thresholds. The range between the reported minimum and maximum adjusted slope coefficients is .011 at the 60 percent, .014 at the 55 percent, and .044 at the 50 percent threshold. The range is fairly small at the 60 and 55 percent thresholds, meaning that the occurrence of litigation has had little, if any, impact on the general relationship. At the 50 percent threshold, however, the presence of litigation does impact the adoption of black minority-opportunity districts in a positive, although modest, fashion.

Last, the modeling of court intervention contributes substantially to the amount of variance in the dependent variable explained for Hispanic cities. The inclusion increases the explained variance from an R^2 of .698 to an adjusted R^2 of .783 for the 60 percent threshold, .622 to .685 for the 55 percent threshold, and .798 to .843 for the 50 percent threshold. For black cities, the amount of variance in the dependent variable explained by the addition of court intervention is mixed. The explained variance decreases from an R^2 of .815 to an adjusted R^2 of .792 for the 60 percent threshold, .829 to .806 for the 55 percent threshold, and increases from .839 to .858 for the 50 percent threshold. Unlike the 60 and 55 percent thresholds, there is a relatively sizable increase in the variance explained at the 50 percent threshold, suggesting the importance of court intervention in the adoption of black minority-opportunity districts at this threshold.

CHAPTER SIX

The Election of Hispanic and Black Descriptive Representatives: Model Testing and Findings

We are now ready to test the second general relationship, the subsequent election of Hispanic and black council members from adopted Hispanic and black minority-opportunity districts, respectively.[1] Also tested are three subhypotheses positing the variables resource disparity, partisan elections, and district population density as conditioning this second general relationship across the three elections subsequent to the 1990 round of redistricting.

Table 6.1 provides the number of cities that adopted at least one minority-opportunity district, the number of minority-opportunity districts adopted, and the number of minorities elected from these districts by minority status (either Hispanic or black) at each voting-age threshold for the three elections subsequent to the 1990 redistricting. For example, at the 50 percent voting-age population threshold, 60 cities have adopted at least one black minority-opportunity district. Among these 60 cities are 181 adopted black minority-opportunity districts. The number of black descriptive representatives elected from these districts is 169 in the first and second elections, and 166 in the third election subsequent to the 1990 round of redistricting. The average number of black minority-opportunity districts per city is 2.88. The average number of black descriptive representatives elected from black minority-opportunity districts per city is 2.81 during the first and second elections, and 2.76 during the third election subsequent to the 1990 round of redistricting.

TABLE 6.1

NUMBER OF CITIES EXAMINED, NUMBER OF DISTRICTS THAT HAVE BEEN ADOPTED AS MINORITY-OPPORTUNITY, AND NUMBER OF ELECTED MINORITY OFFICIALS BY MINORITY STATUS, VOTING-AGE POPULATION THRESHOLD, AND ELECTION

	60% VAP MIN.-OPP. THRESHOLD	55% VAP MIN.-OPP. THRESHOLD	50% VAP MIN.-OPP. THRESHOLD
Hispanic			
Cities (N)	10	16	25
Minority-Opp. Districts (N)	32 [3.00]	40 [2.31]	56 [2.08]
1st Election/Hispanic Officials (N)	27 [2.70]	31 [1.93]	40 [1.60]
2nd Election/Hispanic Officials (N)	27 [2.70]	30 [1.87]	40 [1.60]
3rd Election/Hispanic Officials (N)	27 [2.70]	32 [2.00]	42 [1.68]
Black			
Cities (N)	54	55	60
Minority-Opp. Districts (N)	143 [2.50]	159 [2.74]	181 [2.88]
1st Election/Black Officials (N)	132 [2.44]	148 [2.69]	169 [2.81]
2nd Election/Black Officials (N)	132 [2.44]	148 [2.69]	169 [2.81]
3rd Election/Black Officials (N)	130 [2.40]	136 [2.47]	166 [2.76]

Note: Numbers in brackets are means.

As would be expected, as the threshold decreases, the number of cities increases in analyses for Hispanics and blacks. Cities in the Hispanic analysis-increase from 10 to 16 and then to 25, while cities in the black analysis increase from 54 to 55 and then to 60. In similar fashion, as the threshold decreases the total number of Hispanic minority-opportunity districts increases, and the total number of Hispanic officials elected from these districts increases. Similarly, as the threshold decreases, the total number of black minority-opportunity districts increases, and the total number of black officials elected from these districts increases.

Likewise, for cities in the Hispanic analysis the average number per city of minority-opportunity districts and the average number per city of Hispanic officials elected from these districts (both shown in brackets) decreases as the threshold decreases. In contrast, though, for cities in the black analysis the average number per city of minority-opportunity districts and the average number per city of black officials elected from these districts increases as the threshold decreases.

Tables 6.2a and 6.2b provide descriptive statistics for the variables Hispanic minority-opportunity districts (HOD), Hispanic elected officials (HEO), black minority-opportunity districts (BOD), and black elected officials (BEO) on the metric to be used in the regression equations. The Hispanic or black minority-opportunity districts variable is the *proportion* of a city's districts adopted as either Hispanic or black minority-opportunity. With reference to table 6.2a, on average .415, .342, and .308 of all districts in each city in the Hispanic analysis are adopted as either 60, 55, or 50 percent Hispanic minority-opportunity, respectively. The average proportion of each city's districts adopted as Hispanic minority-opportunity decreases between the 60 and 55 percent thresholds by 17.6 percent (from .415 to .342), and it decreases again between the 55 and 50 percent thresholds by 9.9 percent (from .342 to .308). The standard deviation also decreases as the threshold decreases, from .298 to .282, to .246. This suggests that the variation in the proportion of a city's districts adopted as Hispanic minority-opportunity is greater at the 60 percent threshold relative to the 50 percent threshold.

Contrast these findings with cities in the black analysis. With reference to table 6.2b, on average .293, .326, and .339 of all districts in each black city are adopted as either 60, 55, or 50 percent black minority-opportunity, respectively. The average proportion of each city's districts adopted as black minority-opportunity increase between the 60 and 55 percent thresholds by 11.2 percent (from .293 to .326), and it increases between the 55 and 50 percent thresholds by 3.9 (from .326 to .339).

Note that in comparing Hispanic and black cities in the analyses, the proportion of a city's districts that is minority-opportunity is quite dissimilar. Hispanics, on average, adopt .415, .342, and .308 percent of the available districts, respectively, while blacks, on average, adopt .293, .326, and.339 percent of the available districts, respectively. The standard deviation for cities in the black analysis changes from .189 to .184 to .196 between the 60, 55, and 50 percent thresholds, while those for the cities in the Hispanic analysis change from .298 to .282 to .246 between the 60, 55, and 50 percent thresholds, respectively. This suggests that the variation in the proportion of a city's districts adopted as black minority-opportunity remains, in contrast to the Hispanic variation, roughly unchanged between thresholds.

The Hispanic and black elected officials (HEO and BEO) variables are the respective *proportion* of a city's council that have descriptive representatives elected from minority-opportunity districts. With reference to table 6.2a, on

TABLE 6.2A

PROPORTION OF A CITY'S DISTRICTS THAT HAVE BEEN ADOPTED AS HISPANIC MINORITY-OPPORTUNITY AND PROPORTION OF A CITY'S COUNCIL THAT IS HISPANIC BY VOTING-AGE POPULATION THRESHOLD AND ELECTION

	60% VAP HISP.-OPP. THRESHOLD	55% VAP HISP.-OPP. THRESHOLD	50% VAP HISP.-OPP. THRESHOLD
Hispanic Opportunity-Districts (HOD):			
Mean	.415	.342	.308
Standard Deviation	.298	.282	.246
Cities N	10	16	25
1st Election Hispanic Elected Officials (HEO):			
Mean	.346	.258	.233
Standard Deviation	.292	.265	.227
Cities N	10	16	25
2nd Election Hispanic Elected Officials (HEO):			
Mean	.346	.265	.240
Standard Deviation	.292	.259	.227
Cities N	10	16	25
3rd Election Hispanic Elected Officials (HEO):			
Mean	.346	.271	.240
Standard Deviation	.292	.265	.227
Cities N	10	16	25

average .346 of a city's districted council seats are held by Hispanic descriptive representatives elected from Hispanic minority-opportunity districts following the first election subsequent to the 1990 round of redistricting at the 60 percent threshold. This average decreases to .258 and further to .233 as the threshold decreases. Similar patterns also are found for the second and third elections subsequent to the redistricting. The standard deviation about the mean for Hispanic elected officials during the first election is .292 at the 60 percent threshold, .265 at the 55 percent threshold, and .227 at the 50 percent threshold. Similar patterns are found for the second and third elections.

TABLE 6.2B

PROPORTION OF A CITY'S DISTRICTS THAT HAVE BEEN ADOPTED AS BLACK MINORITY-OPPORTUNITY AND PROPORTION OF A CITY'S COUNCIL THAT IS BLACK BY VOTING-AGE POPULATION THRESHOLD AND ELECTION

	60% VAP BLACK-OPP. THRESHOLD	55% VAP BLACK-OPP. THRESHOLD	50% VAP BLACK-OPP. THRESHOLD
Black Opportunity-Districts (BOD):			
Mean	.293	.326	.339
Standard Deviation	.189	.184	.196
Cities N	54	55	60
1st Election Black Elected Officials (BEO):			
Mean	.256	.287	.299
Standard Deviation	.164	.175	.177
Cities N	54	55	60
2nd Election Black Elected Officials (BEO):			
Mean	.264	.290	.300
Standard Deviation	.174	.175	.179
Cities N	54	55	60
3rd Election Black Elected Officials (BEO):			
Mean	.261	.290	.298
Standard Deviation	.168	.168	.172
Cities N	54	55	60

With reference to table 6.2b, on average .256 of a city's districted council seats are held by black descriptive representatives elected from black minority-opportunity districts in the first election subsequent to the 1990 round of redistricting at the 60 percent threshold. This average increases to .287 and to .299 as the threshold decreases. Similar patterns also are found for the second and third elections subsequent to the redistricting. The standard deviation about the mean for black elected officials is .164 at the 60 percent threshold for the first election, .175 at the 55 percent threshold, and .177 at the 50 percent threshold. Similar patterns are found for the second and third elections.

Our second general hypothesis states that the proportion of a city's council districts that is Hispanic or black minority-opportunity provides an explanation for the proportion of the city's council that has descriptive representatives elected from these Hispanic or black minority-opportunity districts, respectively. Regression is used to test this relationship for the three elections subsequent to the 1990 round of redistricting. The proportion of a city's districts that is Hispanic minority-opportunity is specified as HOD, and the proportion of a city's districts that is black minority-opportunity is specified as BOD. The presence of Hispanic officials elected from Hispanic minority-opportunity districts (as a proportion of all districted elected officials) and the presence of black officials elected from black minority-opportunity districts (as a proportion of all districted elected officials) are specified as HEO and BEO, respectively.

$$HEO_{t..t+2} = a + b1HOD$$
$$BEO_{t..t+2} = a + b1BOD$$

a is the intercept
b is the slope coefficient
t is the time of the election

The predicted value of the dependent variable is dependent upon the intercept as well as the slope coefficient. Assuming an intercept (a) at or near 0, an unstandardized regression coefficient, or slope coefficient (b), approaching 1.0 means that the actual proportion of all districts that are minority-opportunity—either Hispanic or black—tends to be about the same as the proportion of all districted officials elected from minority-opportunity districts that are descriptive representatives, either Hispanic or black. By design, it is not possible for either HEO or BEO to exceed HOD or BOD, respectively. However, a slope coefficient may exceed 1 provided there is a negative intercept.

The findings in table 6.3 show that the proportion of a city's council districts that is Hispanic minority-opportunity explains well the election of Hispanics in the three elections subsequent to the 1990 round of redistricting. At the 60 percent threshold, the slope coefficients for the three elections are all .935, and the intercepts are all -.041. At the 55 percent threshold, the slope coefficients for the three elections are .881, .871, and .860 and the intercepts are -.043, -.032, and -.022, respectively. At the 50 percent threshold, the slope coefficients for the three elections are .847, .831, and .831, and the intercepts are -.027, -.015, and -.015, respectively. At the 60 percent threshold, the proportion of Hispanic elected officials remains identical across the three elections. Simply, the 60 percent Hispanic minority-opportunity districts elected Hispanic descriptive representatives during the first election, and they consistently continued to do so for the two following elections. At the 55 and 50 percent thresholds, the proportion of Hispanic elected officials, while not identical, remains fairly constant across the three elections. Moreover, as the threshold increases, so do the slope coefficients.

TABLE 6.3

REGRESSION COEFFICIENT ESTIMATES FOR THE ELECTION OF HISPANICS DURING THE THREE ELECTIONS FOLLOWING THE 1990 ROUND OF REDISTRICTING BY VAP THRESHOLD

	1ST ELECTION $HEO_t = a + b1HOD$	2ND ELECTION $HEO_{t+1} = a + b1HOD$	3RD ELECTION $HEO_{t+2} = a + b1HOD$
60% Min.-Opp. Districts			
Intercept	-.041 (.049)	-.041 (.049)	-.041 (.049)
Slope Coefficient	.935 (.098)	.935 (.098)	.935 (.098)
R^2	.900	.900	.900
S.E.E.	.092	.092	.092
Cities N	10	10	10
55% Min.-Opp. Districts			
Intercept	-.043 (.037)	-.032 (.034)	-.022 (.034)
Slope Coefficient	.881 (.084)	.871 (.077)	.860 (.077)
R^2	.871	.888	.885
S.E.E.	.095	.086	.087
Cities N	16	16	16
50% Min.-Opp. Districts			
Intercept	-.027 (.030)	-.015 (.033)	-.015 (.033)
Slope Coefficient	.847 (.077)	.831 (.085)	.831 (.085)
R^2	.833	.797	.797
S.E.E.	.092	.102	.102
Cities N	25	25	25

Notes: 1. All coefficients are significant at the .001 level.
2. Numbers in parentheses are standard errors.

Also, the explained variance (R^2) (indicating the fit of the data about the regression line) for the 60 percent threshold is .900 for each of the three elections. For the 55 percent threshold it is .881 for the first election, .871 for the second election, and .860 for the third election. For the 50 percent threshold the explained variance is .833 for the first election, .797 for the second election, and .797 for the third election. As the threshold increases, so does the amount of variance explained across the three elections.

The interpretation of the slope coefficients and intercepts in combination with the explained variances is consistent with theoretical expectations. The larger the proportion of voting-age population that is Hispanic in a district, the higher the probability that a Hispanic descriptive representative will be elected from that district.

The findings in table 6.4 show that the proportion of a city's council districts that is black minority-opportunity explains well the election of blacks in these districts in the three elections subsequent to the 1990 round of redistricting. At the 60 percent threshold, the slope coefficients for the three elections are .785, .859, and .821, and the intercepts are .019, .009, and .012, respectively. At the 55 percent threshold, the slope coefficients for the three elections are .864, .858, and .811, and the intercepts are -.005, -.009, and .012, respectively. At the 50 percent threshold, the slope coefficients for the three thresholds are .827, .826, and .790, and the intercepts are .010, .011, and .016, respectively. At all thresholds, the proportion of black elected officials remains fairly constant across the three elections.

Also, the explained variance (R^2) for the 60 percent threshold is .817 for the first election, .871 for the second election, and .851 for the third election. For the 55 percent threshold the explained variance is .823 for the first election, .828 for the second election, and .797 for the third election. For the 50 percent threshold the explained variance is .828 at the first election, .828 for the second election, and .819 for the third election. Moreover, as the threshold increases between 50 and 55 percent for each election, the amount of explained variance does not increase. Between the 55 and 60 percent thresholds, however, the explained variance increases at the second and third elections.

The proportion of a city's council districts that is minority-opportunity alone may not provide a complete explanation for the proportion of the city's council that has descriptive representatives elected from these minority-opportunity districts. The R^2s leave as much as 15 percent of the variance unexplained for Hispanic elected officials and as much as 33 percent of the variance unexplained for the black elected officials. Our theory suggests that additional variables may contribute to a more complete explanation of the election of Hispanics and blacks from these minority-opportunity districts. They should be introduced as specifying variables that condition this relationship (i.e., modifying the intercept and slope coefficient) rather than introduced as independent variables acting directly on the presence of elected minorities. These three specifying variables are as follows:

RD = Resource Disparity
PE = Partisan Elections
DP = District Population Density

Each specifying variable is included in a regression to measure its conditioning effect on the intercept and slope coefficient.

RESOURCE DISPARITY CONDITIONING THE SECOND GENERAL RELATIONSHIP

Table 6.5 models the impact of resource disparity, which is the ratio of citywide either Hispanic or black median income to the median income of

TABLE 6.4

REGRESSION COEFFICIENT ESTIMATES FOR THE ELECTION OF BLACKS DURING THE THREE ELECTIONS FOLLOWING THE 1990 ROUND OF REDISTRICTING BY VAP THRESHOLD

	1ST ELECTION $BEO_t = a + b1BOD$	2ND ELECTION $BEO_{t+1} = a + b1BOD$	3RD ELECTION $BEO_{t+2} = a + b1BOD$
60% Min.-Opp. Districts			
Intercept	.019 (.018)	.009 (.016)	.012 (.017)
Slope Coefficient	.785 (.051)	.859 (.046)	.821 (.047)
R^2	.817	.871	.851
S.E.E.	.070	.062	.065
Cities N	54	54	54
55% Min.-Opp. Districts			
Intercept	-.005 (.020)	-.009 (.020)	.012 (.021)
Slope Coefficient	.864 (.054)	.858 (.054)	.811 (.056)
R^2	.823	.828	.797
S.E.E.	.073	.072	.076
Cities N	55	55	55
50% Min.-Opp. Districts			
Intercept	.010 (.019)	.011 (.019)	.016 (.019)
Slope Coefficient	.827 (.049)	.826 (.049)	.790 (.049)
R^2	.828	.828	.819
S.E.E.	.073	.074	.073
Cities N	60	60	60

Notes: 1. All coefficients are significant at the .001 level.
2. Numbers in parentheses are standard errors.

non-Hispanic whites, as a specifying variable conditioning the second general relationship. Equations 1 through 3 present the findings at the 60, 55, and 50 percent Hispanic voting-age population thresholds, and equations 4 through 6 present the findings at the 60, 55, and 50 percent black voting-age population thresholds. The dependent variables, the election of Hispanic and black descriptive representatives from the minority-opportunity districts, are examined at times t, t+1, and t+2, representing the three elections subsequent to the 1990 round of redistricting.

The measure of resource disparity has a theoretical range of 0 (indicating the complete absence of disparity in resources), and it approaches 1 (indicating a growing disparity in resources), but the empirical range, reflecting cities

TABLE 6.5

REGRESSION COEFFICIENT ESTIMATES OF THE SPECIFYING VARIABLE RESOURCE DISPARITY ON THE SECOND GENERAL RELATIONSHIP FOR THE THREE ELECTIONS SUBSEQUENT TO THE 1990 ROUND OF REDISTRICTING

	$HEO_{t..t+2}$ = a + b1HOD + b2RD + b3(HOD*RD)									$BEO_{t..t+2}$ = a + b1BOD + b2RD + b3(BOD*RD)								
	EQUATION 1 60% VAP			EQUATION 2 55% VAP			EQUATION 3 50% VAP			EQUATION 4 60% VAP			EQUATION 5 55% VAP			EQUATION 6 50% VAP		
	t	t+1	t+2	t	t+1	t+2	t	t+1	t+2	t	t+1	t+2	t	t+1	t+2	t	t+1	t+2
Intercept	-.001	-.001	-.001	-.089	-.058	-.014	-.010	.028	.028	-.058	-.024	-.027	-.044	.001	-.064	.104	.120	.075
	.237	.237	.237	.150	.133	.134	.102	.120	.120	.073	.071	.072	.103	.103	.107	.088	.090	.090
Min. Opp.	1.14*	1.14*	1.14*	1.33***	1.26***	1.20***	1.31***	1.24***	1.24***	1.16***	1.04***	1.11***	1.05***	.981***	1.12***	.960***	.983***	.998***
District	.330	.330	.330	.412	.356	.134	.302	.356	.356	.176	.169	.171	.235	.232	.240	.201	.203	.203
Resource	-.062	-.062	-.062	.114	.071	.004	-.042	-.140	-.140	.086	.073	.049	.082	-.002	.110	-.216	-.246	-.133
Disparity	.434	.434	.434	.295	.262	.263	.203	.240	.240	.145	.114	.142	.202	.202	.209	.179	.183	.183
H/BOD*RD	-1.01	-1.01	-1.01	-1.72	-1.57	-1.41	-1.76**	-1.64*	-1.64*	-1.00**	-.767**	-.778**	-.545	-.416	-.765	-.146	-.103	-.296
Interaction	1.01	1.01	1.01	.914	.810	.813	.668	.788	.788	.327	.313	.315	.434	.428	.442	.374	.377	.377
N	10	10	10	16	16	16	25	25	25	54	54	54	55	55	55	60	60	60
Adjusted R^2	.913	.913	.913	.901	.919	.917	.905	.868	.868	.864	.896	.886	.831	.839	.814	.853	.855	.843
S.E.E.	.086	.086	.086	.083	.073	.073	.070	.082	.082	.060	.056	.056	.072	.070	.072	.068	.068	.068

Notes: 1. Italicized numbers are standard errors for the unstandardized regression coefficients.
2. * = Significance at .05 level, ** = Significance at .01 level, *** = Significance at .001 level

Regression Coefficient Estimates of the Specifying Variable Resource Disparity on the Second General Relationship for the Three Elections subsequent to the 1990 Round of Redistricting *(Continued)*

	$HEO_{t..t+2}$ = a + b1HOD + b2RD + b3(HOD*RD)									$BEO_{t..t+2}$ = a + b1BOD + b2RD + b3(BOD*RD)								
	EQUATION 1 60% VAP			EQUATION 2 55% VAP			EQUATION 3 50% VAP			EQUATION 4 60% VAP			EQUATION 5 55% VAP			EQUATION 6 50% VAP		
	t	t+1	t+2	t	t+1	t+2	t	t+1	t+2	t	t+1	t+2	t	t+1	t+2	t	t+1	t+2
Opp Dist:																		
Mean	.415	.415	.415	.342	.342	.342	.308	.308	.308	.293	.293	.293	.326	.326	.326	.339	.339	.339
RD Range:																		
1-Std. Dev.	.235	.235	.235	.261	.261	.261	.299	.299	.299	.371	.371	.371	.366	.366	.366	.371	.371	.371
Mean	.412	.412	.412	.418	.418	.418	.451	.451	.451	.506	.506	.506	.502	.502	.502	.502	.502	.502
1-Std. Dev.	.589	.589	.589	.574	.574	.574	.604	.604	.604	.641	.641	.641	.661	.661	.661	.634	.634	.634
Adjustment:																		
For 1-Std. Dev. Below Mean RD:																		
Coeff.	1.04	1.04	1.04	1.17	1.11	1.07	1.14	1.08	1.08	1.05	.956	1.02	.986	.931	1.03	.942	.970	.961
Intercept	-.016	-.016	-.016	-.059	-.039	-.013	-.022	-.015	-.015	-.026	.003	-.008	-.014	-.001	-.023	.024	.029	.025
For Mean RD:																		
Coeff.	.966	.966	.966	1.08	1.03	.996	1.06	1.00	1.00	1.01	.926	.995	.962	.913	.995	.935	.965	.948
Intercept	-.027	-.027	-.027	-.041	-.028	-.013	-.029	-.035	-.035	-.014	.012	-.002	-.003	-.001	-.008	-.004	-.003	.008
For 1-Std. Dev. Above Mean RD:																		
Coeff.	.893	.893	.893	.992	.951	.923	.982	.934	.934	.972	.896	.964	.933	.891	.955	.929	.961	.934
Intercept	-.038	-.038	-.038	-.024	-.017	-.013	-.035	-.057	-.057	-.003	.022	.004	.010	-.001	.008	-.033	-.036	-.009

in the analysis, is truncated within this theoretical range. For example, within the universe of cities that actually adopted one Hispanic minority-opportunity district at the 60 percent voting-age population threshold is found an empirical range that extends from a minimum of .221 (Pomona, Calif.) to a maximum of .694 (Dallas, Tex.). The mean level of resource disparity, however, is .412, and one standard deviation below is .235, and one standard deviation above is .589. The dispersion of resource disparity scores about the mean suggests a considerable amount of variation in resource disparity for cities in both the analyses for Hispanics and blacks. The range between the one standard deviation above and below the mean is similar for both Hispanic and black cities, yet resource disparity tends to be more acute in black than Hispanic cities. The average resource disparity score for Hispanics across the three thresholds is about .427, while for blacks across the three thresholds is about .503.[2]

The effect of introducing resource disparity as an interaction term conditioning the second general relationship is the modification, or adjustment, of the slope coefficient and intercept. The coefficient for the resource disparity variable, reported in the top half of table 6.5, adjusts the intercept, while the coefficient for the interaction term, also reported in the top half of table 6.5, serves as an adjustment in the slope coefficient. Reported in the bottom half of table 6.5 are adjustments in the intercepts and slope coefficients for three different values of resource disparity, specifically the mean and 1 standard deviation above and below the mean when the proportion of districts that are minority-opportunity is set at its average for that group of cities. In addition, reported are these values for the three elections subsequent the 1990 redistricting. Using equation 1 as an example, one that concerns the election of Hispanic descriptive representatives from Hispanic minority-opportunity districts at the 60 percent threshold during the first election following redistricting, a resource disparity score of .235 (one standard deviation below the mean RD score) results in an adjusted slope coefficient of 1.04 and intercept of -.016. A resource disparity score of .589 (one standard deviation above the mean RD score) results in an adjusted slope coefficient of .893 and intercept of -.038, while a resource disparity score of .412 (the mean value) will produce an adjusted slope coefficient of .966 and intercept of -.027.

The findings show the interaction term as significant for each of the three elections subsequent to redistricting for Hispanic cities at the 50 percent threshold and for black cities at the 60 percent threshold. An examination of the lower half of table 6.5 shows that as disparity in resources narrows from one standard deviation above to one standard deviation below the mean, the slope coefficients increase for the cities in both the Hispanic and black analyses. This is consistent with theoretical expectations that as the disparity in resources increases, it will become increasingly difficulty to elect Hispanic descriptive representatives from Hispanic minority-opportunity districts.

The findings show that when resource disparity is relatively high (i.e., at or near one standard deviation above its mean) it impacts adversely on the translation between the proportion of a city's districts that are Hispanic minority-opportunity and the proportion of the council seats held by Hispanic descriptive representatives elected from these districts. When it is relatively low (i.e., at or near one standard deviation below its mean), it impacts more positively the translation.

An examination of the ranges between the reported minimum and maximum adjusted coefficients and the range between the minimum and maximum intercepts allows an assessment of the impact of resource disparity relative to each threshold. For the cities that are 60 percent Hispanic, the average ranges in coefficients and intercepts for the three elections respectively are .147 and .022. For the 55 percent threshold, they are .161 and .019, and for the 50 percent threshold they are .150 and .032, respectively. For the cities in the Hispanic analysis, it may be said first that resource disparity plays a noteworthy role in the election of Hispanic descriptive representatives and, second, that its impact is roughly the same across the three thresholds. For the 60 percent black cities, the average ranges in coefficients and intercepts for the three elections are .065 and .015, respectively. For the 55 percent threshold they are .056 and .011, respectively, and for the 50 percent threshold they are .016 and .032, respectively. Among the black cities the impact of the level of resource disparity is more demonstrative at the 60 and 55 percent thresholds than it is at the 50 percent threshold. Note that the ranges for black cities are much more muted relative to the ranges for Hispanic cities. This clearly suggests that the conditioning effect of resource disparity on the election of minorities is greater for Hispanic cities relative to black cities.

A comparison of the R^2s between table 6.3 and table 6.5 may indicate the contribution to the amount of explained variance in the dependent variable derived from the modeling of Hispanic resource disparity as an interaction. For Hispanics, the R^2 increases about .013 points (from .900 to .913) for each of the three elections at the 60 percent threshold. At the 55 percent threshold, the explained variance increases .030 points (from .871 to .901) for the first election, .031 points (from .888 to .919) for the second election, and .032 points (from .885 to .917) for the third election. At the 50 percent threshold, the explained variance increases .072 points (from .833 to .905) for the first election, and .071 points (from .797 to .868) for the second and third elections. Notice that the size of the increase in R^2 is largest at the 50 percent threshold, and the size of the increase is smallest at the 60 percent threshold. This suggests that the contribution due to the introduction of resource disparity is greatest at the 50 percent threshold. This is theoretically sound. As a district's overall voting-age population becomes increasingly Hispanic, the less likely resource disparity will condition the election of Hispanic descriptive representatives. In simple terms, sheer numbers can overcome deficits in resources.

Likewise, a comparison of the R^2s in table 6.4 and table 6.5 may indicate the contribution to the amount of explained variance in the dependent variable derived from the modeling of black resource disparity as an interaction. For blacks at the 60 percent threshold, the R^2 increases .047 points (from .817 to .864) for the first election, .026 (from .871 to .896) for the second election, and .035 (from .851 to .886) for the third election. At the 55 percent threshold, the explained variance increases .008 points (from .823 to .831) for the first election, .011 points (from .828 to .839) for the second election, and .017 points (from .797 to .814) for the third election. At the 50 percent threshold, the explained variance increases .025 points (from .828 to .853) for the first election, .027 points (from .828 to .855) for the second election, and .024 points (from .819 to .843) for the third election. The increase in R^2s for blacks at each threshold is a mere several points suggesting that the contribution due to the introduction of resource disparity is, at best, modest across all thresholds.

PARTISANSHIP CONDITIONING THE SECOND GENERAL RELATIONSHIP

In a similar fashion, table 6.6 models the conditioning effect of partisan elections on the relationship between the proportion of a city's council districts that is either Hispanic or black minority-opportunity and the proportion of districted council members that is either Hispanic or black officials elected from these respective districts. Equations 1 through 3 present the findings at the 60, 55, and 50 percent Hispanic voting-age population thresholds, and equations 4 through 6 present the findings at the 60, 55, and 50 percent black voting-age population thresholds. The dependent variables, reflecting the election of Hispanic and black descriptive representatives from their respective minority-opportunity districts as a proportion of all districts, are examined at times t, t+1, and t+2, representing the three elections subsequent to the 1990 round of redistricting.

The variable partisan elections is handled as a dichotomous measure with those cities having partisan elections coded 1 and those with nonpartisan elections coded 0. The effect of introducing partisan elections as an interaction term conditioning the second general relationship is the modification, or adjustment, of the slope coefficient and intercept. Changes in the intercepts and slope coefficients are reported in the bottom half of table 6.6. Findings are not reported for Hispanic cities at the 60 percent and 55 percent thresholds due to a lack of variance in the partisan elections variable (i.e., partisan elections were present in 90 percent and 87.5 percent of cities, respectively). Using equation 3 as an example, one that concerns the election of Hispanic descriptive representatives from Hispanic minority-opportunity districts at the 50 percent threshold during the first election following redistricting, the slope coefficient is .866 and the intercept is -.016 for nonpartisan cities, while they are .834 and -.070 for cities with partisan elections. The .032 drop in the value of the coefficient and .054 decrease in the intercept when moving from minimum PE to maximum PE suggests that the presence of partisan election impacts adversely the election of Hispanic descriptive representatives.

The findings show the interaction term as significant for the three elections subsequent to redistricting for black cities in the analysis at the 60 percent threshold. An examination of the lower half of table 6.6 shows that the presence of partisan elections decreases the slope coefficient while increasing the intercepts for the cities in the black analysis. At the 60 percent threshold, the slope coefficients decrease an average of .075, and the intercepts increase an average of .060. At the 55 percent threshold, the slope coefficients decrease an average of .062, and the intercepts increase an average of .046. At the 50 percent threshold, the slope coefficients decrease an average of .020, and the intercepts increase an average of .008. This means, contrary to theoretical expectations, that the presence of partisan elections impacts the election of blacks adversely, although the impact is slight. Also, with reference to the impact of partisan elections relative to each threshold, it may be said that partisan elections are more demonstrative for cities in the 60 percent threshold analysis relative to cities in the 55 percent threshold analysis, and, again, relative to cities in the 50 percent threshold analysis.

A comparison of the R^2s in table 6.3 and table 6.6 may indicate the contribution to the amount of explained variance in the dependent variable derived from the modeling of partisan elections as an interaction in the Hispanic analysis. For cities in the Hispanic analysis at the 50 percent threshold, the explained variance remains largely unchanged, decreasing .013 points (from .833 to .824) at the first election and increasing .004 points (from .797 to .801) at the second and third elections. Likewise, a comparison of the R^2s between table 6.4 and table 6.6 may indicate the contribution for cities in the black analysis. For these cities at the 60 percent threshold, the R^2 increases .022 points (from .817 to .839) for the first election, .006 (from .871 to .877) for the second election, and .014 (from .851 to .865) for the third election. At the 55 percent threshold, the explained variance remains the same (from .823 to .823) for the first election, increases .001 points (from .828 to .829) for the second election, and increases .009 points (from .797 to .806) for the third election. At the 50 percent threshold, the explained variance decreases .005 points (from .828 to .823) for the first and second elections and decreases .001 points (from .819 to .818) for the third election. The change in R^2s for both groups of cities, at each threshold, is negligible, suggesting that there is no substantive contribution due to the introduction of the partisan elections variable.

DISTRICT POPULATION DENSITY CONDITIONING THE SECOND GENERAL RELATIONSHIP

The third and final variable, modeled in table 6.7, is district population density, the physical density of the population in the minority-opportunity district. Equations 1 through 3 present the findings at the 60, 55, and 50 percent

TABLE 6.6

REGRESSION COEFFICIENT ESTIMATES OF THE SPECIFYING VARIABLE PARTISAN ELECTIONS ON THE SECOND GENERAL RELATIONSHIP FOR THE THREE ELECTIONS SUBSEQUENT TO THE 1990 ROUND OF REDISTRICTING

	$HEO_{t..t+2}$ = a + b1HOD + b2PE + b3(HOD*PE)									$BEO_{t..t+2}$ = a + b1BOD + b2PE + b3(BOD*PE)								
	EQUATION 1 60% VAP			EQUATION 2 55% VAP			EQUATION 3 50% VAP			EQUATION 4 60% VAP			EQUATION 5 55% VAP			EQUATION 6 50% VAP		
	t	t+1	t+2	t	t+1	t+2	t	t+1	t+2	t	t+1	t+2	t	t+1	t+2	t	t+1	t+2
Intercept	—	—	—	—	—	—	-.016	-.010	-.010	-.023	-.023	-.023	-.023	-.023	-.024	.016	.016	.016
	—	—	—	—	—	—	.116	.123	.123	.027	.025	.025	.033	.032	.033	.031	.031	.030
Min. Opp. District	—	—	—	—	—	—	.866	1.07	1.07	1.00***	1.00***	1.00***	.971***	.971***	.971***	.851***	.851***	.854***
	—	—	—	—	—	—	.746	.794	.794	.087	.080	.081	.094	.093	.095	.081	.081	.079
Partisan Elections	—	—	—	—	—	—	-.054	-.060	-.060	.072*	.048	.061	.041	.048	.072	.003	.003	.019
	—	—	—	—	—	—	.121	.129	.129	.034	.032	.033	.042	.041	.042	.040	.040	.039
H/BOD*PE Interaction	—	—	—	—	—	—	-.102	-.207	-.207	-.306**	-.201*	-.256**	-.159	-.169	-.240	-.036	-.038	-.100
	—	—	—	—	—	—	.751	.799	.799	.104	.097	.098	.116	.114	.117	.102	.103	.101
N	—	—	—	—	—	—	25	25	25	54	54	54	55	55	55	60	60	60
Adjusted R^2	—	—	—	—	—	—	.824	.801	.801	.839	.877	.865	.823	.829	.806	.823	.822	.818
S.E.E.	—	—	—	—	—	—	.095	.101	.101	.065	.061	.062	.073	.072	.074	.074	.075	.073

Notes: 1. Italicized numbers are standard errors for the unstandardized regression coefficients.
2. * = Significance at .05 level, ** = Significance at .01 level, *** = Significance at .001 level

Regression Coefficient Estimates of the Specifying Variable Partisan Elections on the Second General Relationship for the Three Elections subsequent to the 1990 Round of Redistricting *(Continued)*

	$HEO_{t..t+2}$ = a + b1HOD + b2PE + b3(HOD*PE)									$BEO_{t..t+2}$ = a + b1BOD + b2PE + b3(BOD*pE)								
	EQUATION 1 60% VAP			EQUATION 2 55% VAP			EQUATION 3 50% VAP			EQUATION 4 60% VAP			EQUATION 5 55% VAP			EQUATION 6 50% VAP		
	t	t+1	t+2	t	t+1	t+2	t	t+1	t+2	t	t+1	t+2	t	t+1	t+2	t	t+1	t+2
Opp Dist:																		
Mean	—	—	—	—	—	—	.308	.308	.308	.293	.293	.293	.326	.326	.326	.339	.339	.339
PE Range:																		
Minimum	—	—	—	—	—	—	0	0	0	0	0	0	0	0	0	0	0	0
Maximum	—	—	—	—	—	—	1	1	1	1	1	1	1	1	1	1	1	1
Adjustment:																		
For Min PE:																		
Coeff.	—	—	—	—	—	—	.866	1.07	1.07	1.00	1.00	1.00	.971	.971	.971	.851	.851	.854
Intercept	—	—	—	—	—	—	-.016	-.010	-.010	-.023	-.023	-.023	-.023	-.023	-.024	.016	.016	.016
For Max PE:																		
Coeff.	—	—	—	—	—	—	.834	1.01	1.01	.910	.941	.924	.919	.915	.892	.838	.838	.820
Intercept	—	—	—	—	—	—	-.070	-.070	-.070	.049	.025	.038	.018	.025	.027	.019	.019	.035

Table 6.7

Regression Coefficient Estimates of the Specifying Variable District Population Density on the Second General Relationship for the Three Elections subsequent to the 1990 Round of Redistricting

	$HEO_{t..t+2}$ = a + b1HOD + b2DP + b3(HOD*DP)									$BEO_{t..t+2}$ = a + b1BOD + b2DP + b3(BOD*DP)								
	EQUATION 1 60% VAP			EQUATION 2 55% VAP			EQUATION 3 50% VAP			EQUATION 4 60% VAP			EQUATION 5 55% VAP			EQUATION 6 50% VAP		
	t	t+1	t+2	t	t+1	t+2	t	t+1	t+2	t	t+1	t+2	t	t+1	t+2	t	t+1	t+2
Intercept	-.147	-.147	-.147	-.046	-.029	-.014	-.019	.002	.002	.029	.017	.023	-.006	-.001	.015	.004	.005	.015
	.057	.057	.057	.054	.048	.047	.048	.053	.053	.024	.021	.022	.025	.025	.026	.024	.024	.024
	***	***	***	***	***	***	***	***	***	***	***	***	***	***	***	***	***	***
Min.-Opp.	1.17	1.17	1.17	.962	.954	.939	.864	.828	.828	.744	.794	.768	.923	.918	.868	.893	.891	.857
District	.165	.165	.165	.160	.141	.140	.147	.161	.161	.080	.071	.074	.068	.067	.071	.063	.063	.062
District Pop.	.089	.089	.089	.003	.001	.000	-.001	-.005	-.005	-.003	-.007	-.005	.007	.007	.006	.009	.009	.009
Density	.034	.034	.034	.014	.012	.012	.012	.014	.014	.011	.010	.010	.010	.010	.010	.009	.009	.009
H/BOD*DP	-.182	-.182	-.182	-.033	-.035	-.034	-.009	-.002	-.002	.031	.050	.041	-.038	-037	-.035	-.042	-.042	-.043
Interaction	.074	.074	.074	.054	.047	.047	.049	.053	.053	.046	.041	.042	.027	.027	.028	.025	.026	.025
N	10	10	10	16	16	16	25	25	25	54	54	54	55	55	55	60	60	60
Adjusted R^2	.935	.935	.935	.860	.886	.886	.821	.785	.785	.814	.872	.850	.825	.831	.800	.832	.832	.825
S.E.E.	.074	.074	.074	.099	.087	.086	.096	.105	.105	.070	.062	.065	.073	.072	.075	.072	.073	.071

Notes: 1. Italicized numbers are standard errors for the unstandardized regression coefficients.
2. * = Significance at .05 level, ** = Significance at .01 level, *** = Significance at .001 level

Regression Coefficient Estimates of the Specifying Variable District Population Density on the Second General Relationship for the Three Elections subsequent to the 1990 Round of Redistricting *(Continued)*

	$HEO_{t..t+2}$ = a + b1HOD + b2DP + b3(HOD*DP)									$BEO_{t..t+2}$ = a + b1BOD + b2DP + b3(BOD*DP)								
	EQUATION 1 60% VAP			EQUATION 2 55% VAP			EQUATION 3 50% VAP			EQUATION 4 60% VAP			EQUATION 5 55% VAP			EQUATION 6 50% VAP		
	t	t+1	t+2	t	t+1	t+2	t	t+1	t+2	t	t+1	t+2	t	t+1	t+2	t	t+1	t+2
Opp. Dist:																		
Mean	.415	.415	.415	.342	.342	.342	.308	.308	.308	.293	.293	.293	.326	.326	.326	.339	.339	.339
DP Range:																		
1-Std. Dev. ◆	.002	.002	.002	.002	.002	.002	.001	.001	.001	.001	.001	.001	.001	.001	.001	.001	.001	.001
Mean	.018	.018	.018	.033	.033	.033	.030	.030	.030	.016	.016	.016	.017	.017	.017	.017	.017	.017
1-Std. Dev.	.037	.037	.037	.070	.070	.070	.064	.064	.064	.038	.038	.038	.040	.040	.040	.038	.038	.038
Adjustment: For 1-Std. Dev. Below Mean DP:																		
Coeff.	1.23	1.23	1.23	.962	.954	.939	.864	.828	.828	.744	.794	.768	.923	.918	.868	.893	.891	.857
Intercept	-.147	-.147	-.147	-.046	-.029	-.014	-.019	.002	.002	.029	.017	.023	-.006	-.001	.015	.004	.005	.015
For Mean DP:																		
Coeff.	1.23	1.23	1.23	.962	.954	.939	.864	.828	.828	.744	.794	.768	.923	.918	.868	.893	.891	.857
Intercept	-.145	-.145	-.145	-.046	-.029	-.014	-.019	.002	.002	.029	.017	.023	-.006	-.001	.015	.004	.005	.015
For 1-Std. Dev Above Mean DP:																		
Coeff.	1.23	1.23	1.23	.961	.953	.938	.864	.828	.828	.744	.795	.768	.923	.918	.868	.892	.890	.856
Intercept	-.144	-.144	-.144	-.046	-.029	-.014	-.019	.022	.022	.029	.017	.023	-.006	-.001	.015	.004	.005	.01

◆ For the DP Range, one standard deviation below the mean has been truncated to the real-world minimum.

Hispanic voting-age population thresholds, and equations 4 through 6 present the findings at the 60, 55, and 50 percent black voting-age population thresholds. The dependent variables, reflecting the election of Hispanic and black descriptive representatives from their respective minority-opportunity districts as a proportion of all districts, are examined at times t, t+1, and t+2, representing the three elections subsequent to the 1990 round of redistricting.

The measure of district population density has a theoretical range approaching 0 (indicating the near absence of density) and increasing toward 1 (indicating a highly dense environment), but the empirical range, reflecting cities in the analysis, is truncated within this theoretical range. For example, within the universe of cities that actually have adopted one Hispanic minority-opportunity district at the 55 percent threshold, the mean level of district population density is .033; one standard deviation below this is .002, and one standard deviation above this is .070. Both the mean and the range between one standard deviation above and one standard deviation below the mean are greater for the cities in the Hispanic analysis than they are for the cities in the black analysis. This suggests that Hispanics tend to reside in districts with a higher district population density relative to blacks.

It is hypothesized that the introduction of district population density as an interaction term will condition the second general relationship by modifying, or adjusting, the slope coefficient and intercept. Reported in the bottom half of table 6.7 are these adjustments. Counter to expectation, the findings show that the slope coefficients and the intercepts for district population density change very little, if at all, within the range from one standard deviation below to one standard deviation above the mean for both the Hispanic and black analyses. This means that whether district population density is low or high, it has minimal, if any, impact on the translation between the proportion of a city's districts that is minority-opportunity and the proportion of a city's council that is either Hispanic or black officials elected from the respective Hispanic or black minority-opportunity districts. In addition, comparisons of R^2s in tables 6.3 and 6.7 and tables 6.4 and 6.7 show that the addition of district population density does not contribute to the explanation of the election of Hispanics or blacks from minority-opportunity districts at any of the thresholds or elections.

With these findings in mind, we now turn to our concluding chapter, where we discuss the implications of our findings as well as how we conceive and define "meaningful opportunities" to elect candidates of preference.

CHAPTER SEVEN

Conclusion: The Meaning of Meaningful Electoral Opportunity

The intent of this work is both to contribute to an explanation for the creation of minority-opportunity districts at the municipal level and to posit an explanation of the election of minorities from these districts. Endeavoring to explain the adoption of opportunity districts includes theorizing about the role of contextual conditions such as the ability to sell such districts politically, the behavior of incumbents involved in drawing and/or approving such districts, the presence of exogenous scrutiny of the local redistricting process by the federal government in the form of Department of Justice interpretations of congressional statutes and judicial rulings, and the incidence of past litigation stemming from plaintiffs' claims of violations of federal law. The second intent of this research is to provide a more detailed understanding of the conditions under which minorities are elected from these minority-opportunity districts. This endeavor includes an examination of politically relevant resources, whether elections are partisan or not, and the population density of districts.

Summary of Findings for the First General Relationship

For cities in the Hispanic and black analyses, the simple mathematical ability to construct potential minority-opportunity districts independent of political or geographic constraints, identified as system aptitude, are quite similar. For Hispanic cities in the analysis and black cities in the analysis the average proportion (and standard deviation) of a city's districts that may be theoretically minority-opportunity are alike. What is striking is that the proportion of a city's districts that, in practice, are actually adopted as minority-opportunity, on average, is much larger for cities in the black analysis relative to those in the Hispanic analysis. These differences in adoption rates may not be accounted for simply by stating that Hispanic cities are different than black cities in the size of their minority populations or number of council seats—we know these to be similar. This suggests that the political and geographic conditions present in Hispanic cities under analysis must necessarily be different from those in black cities under analysis. This is a significant finding in itself and lends credence to our efforts to identify the conditions that enhance the probability of adoption in Hispanic versus black cities.

One of these conditions is political tenability, the ability to sustain or defend politically the proposition of minority-opportunity districts. Through a historical confluence of statutory law, court rulings, tradition and custom, and culture of political cynicism, there is a visceral caution surrounding districts that are not pleasing to the eye in their simplicity and parsimony. In general, the more odd-shaped a proposed electoral district, the more suspicious one may become about the latent motives or intentions embodied in the rugged, puzzle-shaped contours. It is reasonable to assert that critical commentary is sure to advertise the contrasting demographic differences between districts within a proposed districting plan. A districting plan with ethnic or racial imbalances between districts and hyper-faceted boundaries is a target for charges of racial gerrymandering. The geographic condition of a residentially concentrated, or segregated, minority population enhances the probability of the districting plan containing minority-opportunity districts that have the appearance of compactness and parsimony. These minority-opportunity districts may receive a vigorous defense to charges that the predominant motive falls under the politically inflammatory banner of ethnicity or race.

The findings reveal that Hispanic cities in the analysis have lower levels of segregation relative to black cities in the analysis. On its face this seems to comport with the general finding that the there is a higher translation rate between system aptitude and actual adoption of minority-opportunity districts for black cities relative to Hispanic cities. In fact, it was empirically demonstrated that, for both black and Hispanic cities, this translation is conditioned by segregation: cities with low segregation have a decreased proportion of their council's districts adopted as minority-opportunity relative to when segregation is high. For Hispanic cities and black cities segregation tends to have a greater impact when the threshold for minority-opportunity districts is set at 60 percent rather than 55 or 50 percent minority voting-age population, although the impact is more demonstrative for Hispanic cities relative to black cities. This means that segregation increasingly plays a role in the probability that minority-opportunity districts will be adopted depending on the threshold definition of what constitutes a minority-opportunity district. In short, even with the numerical ability to create a minority-opportunity district, it is unlikely that a minority-opportunity district at the 60 percent threshold will be adopted without the presence of substantial segregation. In turn, segregation as a condition is not as necessary for the adoption of minority-opportunity districts at the 50 percent threshold.

Some may see irony in the connection between increasing segregation and the adoption of minority-opportunity districts. Elevated levels of residential segregation, viewed as the residue, or perhaps the more current by-product, of discrimination and truncated options, is a necessary condition for electoral opportunity by means of adoption of minority-opportunity districts; and those cities that have managed modest minority integration—yet to the naked eye are undeniably still very much segregated—are more likely to be denied electoral opportunity. Others may argue that declining segregation is, in itself, an indication of the progress we have made as a color-blind society and occurs, appropriately, concurrent with a decline in the adoption minority-opportunity districts.

Another condition we found to affect the translation between system aptitude and the actual adoption of minority-opportunity districts is vested minority incumbent advocacy, indicated by the presence of a minority incumbent in conjunction with minority underrepresentation at the time of redistricting. The findings show that districted Hispanic incumbency combined with Hispanic underrepresentation impacts positively on the translation between system aptitude and the actual adoption of Hispanic minority-opportunity districts at each threshold level. In fact, the impact is largest when 60 percent Hispanic minority-opportunity districts are sought. In contrast, black incumbency combined with black underrepresentation is found not to condition the translation. What may account for these Hispanic-black differences? The absence of a relationship for blacks may suggest that either the districted incumbent is not behaving as a strong advocate or that among the remaining members on the council, and perhaps within the community, there is strong opposition to an increase in the number of black minority-opportunity districts.

Divested minority incumbent advocacy—the absence or presence of an at-large minority council member or members at the time of redistricting—also conditions the translation between system aptitude and the actual adoption of minority-opportunity districts. However, contrary to expectation, the presence of an at-large Hispanic official at the time of redistricting slightly decreases the likelihood for the adoption of Hispanic minority-opportunity districts. Clearly, Hispanic at-large incumbents are not vociferous advocates for expanding the number of Hispanic minority-opportunity districts as a means of building potential Hispanic voting coalitions on the city councils. Perhaps this nature of the representative is a reflection of the at-large format. The process of running successfully in an at-large contest requires adept coalition building with non-Hispanics. Potential Hispanic descriptive representatives who either would run ethnically polarized campaigns or would stress the role of ethnicity in policy decisions once elected may be filtered out. In addition, perhaps Hispanic descriptive representation stemming from a citywide contest signals the declining centrality of ethnicity in politics, and therefore, the rationale for proposing or adopting Hispanic minority-opportunity districts is lost. In contrast, the presence of an at-large black descriptive representative at the time of redistricting enhances the probability of the adoption of black minority-opportunity districts. Simply, black at-large incumbents appear to be stronger advocates for the creation of minority-opportunity districts than are at-large Hispanic incumbents. These Hispanic-black differences may not be that surprising when considering the different civil rights–related struggles of the two groups. Black political figures may stress the centrality of elections and election systems as *the* road to the incorporation of black policy preferences.

Scrutiny of the local election process by the federal government in the form of coverage by section 4(b) or section 4(f) of the Voting Rights Act also has been posited as conditioning the relationship between system aptitude and the adoption of minority-opportunity districts. Although there is a strong theoretical expectation that this will hold true, the findings do not substantiate this. For Hispanic cities in the analysis, preclearance coverage impacts this translation in a positive, yet quite weak, fashion. In fact, no additional variance in the dependent variable is explained by the addition of preclearance as an interaction variable. For black cities in the analysis preclearance coverage does not increase the adoption of black minority-opportunity districts relative to black cities not covered by preclearance. That cities within covered jurisdictions are no more likely to adopt minority-opportunity districts than those not covered is a significant finding. The role of federal oversight, at least via the preclearance mechanism, in contributing to the creation of minority-opportunity districts and the election of minorities has been limited at best. This supports our general thesis that the dynamics of local districting is different from districting at the state level in important ways. In contrast with the intrusion preclearance has made in congressional and state redistricting, cities appear to remain more insulated and less responsive to federal government oversight than previously thought.

Court intervention—the presence or absence of voting rights–related litigation in the decade prior to redistricting—also has been posited to condition the relationship between system aptitude and the adoption of minority-opportunity districts. The findings show that the presence of past litigation impacts positively this translation for Hispanic cities and black cities in the analyses. For Hispanic cities, the impact is substantial and consistent across all three thresholds. This means that—independent of the level of threshold for Hispanic minority-opportunity districts—litigation increases the probability for the adoption of Hispanic minority-opportunity districts. Simply, litigation appears to be a successful strategy. For black cities, the findings are mixed. The impact of litigation is substantial at the 50 percent threshold, yet it is absent at the 55 or 60 percent thresholds. This means that the presence of past litigation tends to result in an increase in 50 percent black minority-opportunity districts, but these districts, due to the slight majority nature, are assumed to provide the least opportunity to elect black descriptive representatives. It appears that the response to litigation has not been, as popular impression would have it, the adoption of districts with a heavy preponderance of black residents. Given the presence of past litigation, there tends to be more resistance to the adoption of black, relative to Hispanic, minority-opportunity districts.

These findings are summarized in table 7.1.

TABLE 7.1

SUMMARY OF FINDINGS FOR VARIABLES CONDITIONING THE FIRST GENERAL RELATIONSHIP

CONDITIONING VARIABLE	HISPANIC CITIES (FINDINGS)	BLACK CITIES (FINDINGS)
Political Tenability	1. Strong positive relationship. 2. Higher threshold, larger impact.	1. Strong positive relationship. 2. Higher threshold, larger impact.
Vested Minority Incumbent Advocacy	1. Strong positive relationship. 2. Higher threshold, larger impact.	1. Does not condition the relationship.
Divested Minority Incumbent Advocacy	1. Weak negative relationship. 2. Consistent across thresholds.	1. Strong positive relationship. 2. Consistent across thresholds.
Preclearance	1. Does not condition the relationship.	1. Does not condition the relationship.
Court Intervention	1. Strong positive relationship. 2. Consistent across thresholds.	1. Strong positive relationship at the 50% threshold. 2. Does not condition the relationship at the 55% or 60% thresholds.

SUMMARY OF FINDINGS FOR SECOND GENERAL RELATIONSHIP

The second general relationship posits that the proportion of a city's council districts that is either Hispanic or black minority-opportunity provides an explanation for the proportion of the city's council that has either Hispanic or black descriptive representatives elected from these districts, respectively. We know that many Hispanic and black minority opportunity districts at each threshold have been in fact proposed and adopted. Among these minority-opportunity districts, many have elected descriptive representatives. Yet other minority-opportunity districts have not produced descriptive representatives. The question now becomes: What explains the variation in the presence or absence of descriptive representatives from existing minority-opportunity districts? We have theorized that this variation may be explained, in part, by several conditioning variables.

One of these conditions is resource disparity, the difference in either Hispanic or black median income relative to the median income of non-Hispanic whites. The findings show that as disparity in resources increases, it becomes increasingly less likely that Hispanics will be elected from the Hispanic minority-opportunity districts. The impact of resource disparity is noteworthy across all three thresholds, its impact being greatest at the 50 percent threshold. This suggests that as the proportion of a district's voting-age population becomes increasingly Hispanic, the impact of disparity in resources, although important, becomes relatively less so. Those cities with relatively low resource disparity require a lower threshold of Hispanic voting-age population to assure the opportunity to elect a Hispanic official. Likewise, those cities with a relatively large disparity in resources may require a higher Hispanic voting-age population threshold to assure the opportunity to elect a Hispanic official. For cities in the black analysis, resource disparity also conditions the relationship consistently across the thresholds, although it is much more muted relative to Hispanic cities. Simply, for black cities resources do contribute to the election of blacks, but the assistance is marginal. These findings may have important policy implications for courts and redistricters alike by suggesting that the concept of what constitutes opportunity for Hispanics may have to be broadened to include not just the size of the voting-age population but also a closer look at the relative wealth of the communities. In addition, including relative wealth in defining opportunity for black communities may not be nearly as critical as it is for defining Hispanic opportunity.

Partisan elections also have been proffered as conditioning the translation between minority-opportunity districts and the election of districted minority officials. It has been theorized that the presence of partisan elections will contribute to the election of minority officials by allowing the contest to be framed in terms of party competition rather than the ethnicity or race of the candidates. Contrary to this expectation, the findings reveal that for cities in the Hispanic analysis, the presence of partisan elections impacts adversely the election of Hispanic officials from Hispanic minority-opportunity districts, although data are available only at the 50 percent threshold. Likewise, the presence of partisan elections impacts adversely the election of black officials from black minority-opportunity districts. Within both Hispanic and black cities, the conditioning effect is quite weak, however.

Another condition proposed to affect the translation between minority-opportunity districts and the election of districted minority officials is district population density, the physical density of the population within the minority-opportunity district. It has been theorized that the more spread out the potential voters, the better organized and better financed minority candidates must be in order to contact voters and garner the visibility necessary to win an election. Contrary to expectations, the findings show that for both Hispanic cities and black cities in the analyses the density of district population does not condition the election of minority officials.

These findings are summarized in table 7.2.

TABLE 7.2

SUMMARY OF FINDINGS FOR VARIABLES CONDITIONING THE SECOND GENERAL RELATIONSHIP

CONDITIONING VARIABLE	HISPANIC CITIES (FINDINGS)	BLACK CITIES (FINDINGS)
Resource Disparity	1. Strong positive relationship. 2. Smaller threshold, larger impact. 3. Consistent across all three elections.	1. Weak positive relationship. 2. Consistent across all three thresholds.
Partisan Elections	1. Weak negative relationship. 2. Data only at the 50% threshold. 3. Consistent across all three elections.	1. Weak negative relationship. 2. Consistent across all three elections.
District Population Density	1. Does not condition the relationship.	1. Does not condition the relationship.

MEANINGFUL OPPORTUNITY

An important assumption of this research is that minority-opportunity districts are a precondition for the election of Hispanics and blacks to city councils. What percentage minority, specifically, ought a minority-opportunity district be is still a central issue in many current voting-rights controversies. Recognizing that there is not a consensus, yet consistent with much social science literature as well as several court interpretations, this research chose to investigate the election of minority descriptive representatives from minority-opportunity districts identified as either 50, 55, or 60 percent minority voting-age population. Our findings have illustrated the varying impacts of conditioning variables dependent on the threshold employed.

Within the cities in this study there are Hispanic and black council members elected from single-member districts that are *not* minority-opportunity as we have defined it. In addition, other cities that employ the single-member district format, but do not have enough minorities to theoretically construct a single minority-opportunity district, also have minorities elected to their councils. While a sizable minority population and minority-opportunity districts are unquestionably helpful in the election of descriptive representatives, the question remains: Are minority-opportunity districts the *sine qua non* in defining opportunity, or may opportunity also present itself without these districts and, indeed, without a sizable minority population?

In an effort to shed light on this question, we have decided to perform several additional analyses beyond that which have already been presented. In these analyses we do not assign an a priori definition for *minority-opportunity* in the form of a threshold percent minority population; we simply calculate the probability of electing a Hispanic or black official from a city council district based on the percent of the district that is of Hispanic or black voting-age. These additional analyses include cities with more than 150,000 total population that elect council members by single-member districts. Cities with single-member districts as part of a mixed election system also are included within the analysis concerning only the districted portion of the system. There are 963 districts—the unit of analysis used to calculate the probabilities—derived from 111 cities.[1]

The findings, reported in figures 7.1 and 7.2 below, show that the probability of electing a Hispanic or black council member does not increase proportionately with an increase in said minority's share of the voting-age population. Rather, both Hispanics and blacks remain underrepresented proportionately when their populations are small and are overrepresented proportionately when their populations are large. The probability of electing Hispanics from districts with 25 percent Hispanic voting-age populations is 11 percent, 55 percent probability from districts with 50 percent Hispanic voting-age populations, and 92 percent probability from districts with 75 percent Hispanic voting-age populations. The probability of electing blacks from districts with 25 percent black voting-age populations is 19 percent, 80 percent for districts with 50 percent black voting-age populations, and 98 percent for districts with 75 percent black voting-age populations.

These figures illustrate several important differences between probabilities of electing Hispanics relative to blacks. Hispanics tend to be proportionately underrepresented when their district population is approximately 44.5 percent or less and overrepresented when the population is above this point. Simply, as Hispanics approach numeric majority within districts, so does the probability of electing a Hispanic. On the other hand, black cities, on average, tend to be proportionately underrepresented when black district population is approximately 30 percent or less and show overrepresentation when the population is above this point. Blacks, relative to Hispanics, tend to be proportionately overrepresented well before their population reaches the 50 percent threshold.

FIGURE 7.1

PROBABILITY OF ELECTING A DISTRICTED HISPANIC COUNCIL MEMBER BASED ON THE PERCENTAGE OF THE DISTRICT'S RESIDENTS THAT ARE OF HISPANIC VOTING-AGE

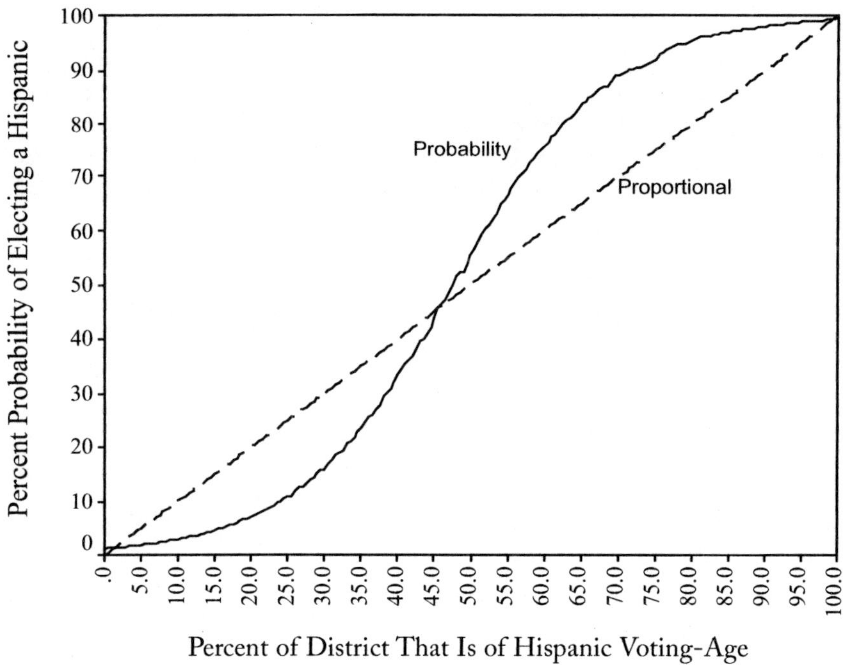

On the one hand, the general curvilinear "s" path of the plotted probabilities is not surprising. It is already well established that single-member districts tend to proportionally overrepresent cohesive voting majorities, while proportionally underrepresenting cohesive voting minorities (e.g., Duverge 1951). What is surprising, however, is the extent to which minorities, especially blacks, are elected from districts that do not have a majority minority population. There is a perception that the election of minorities from nonminority districts is a rare event. And indeed, when we consider congressional and, perhaps, state offices it is in fact a fairly unusual event to have a minority representing a nonminority district. When it does happen, though, it is often presented as an exception, the result of a fluke of circumstances, the result of fractured opposition, or merely the result of the extraordinary charisma of the individual representative. But the data here indicate that at the local level the election of minorities in these districts, while certainly not proportionate, is far from unlikely. For both blacks and Hispanics, when the districted minority population is in the teens as a percent, the opportunity to elect a descriptive representative is truncated. But for blacks, the ability to overcome a deficit in population occurs well before the population reaches 50 percent. This severely challenges the notion of a hard minority threshold of 50 percent black VAP below which minorities have not a reasonable opportunity to elect candidates of preference. Clearly, there is opportunity to elect black descriptive representatives at the city level when the black voting-age population is 5, 10, or even 15 percent below numeric majority. Hispanics do not reach proportional opportunity until the population reaches 45.5 percent, but even below this the curve is fairly shallow indicating that districts with, say, 30, 35 or 40 percent Hispanic VAP still have in practice presented the opportunity to elect Hispanic descriptive representatives.

FIGURE 7.2

PROBABILITY OF ELECTING A DISTRICTED BLACK COUNCIL MEMBER BASED ON THE PERCENTAGE OF THE DISTRICT'S RESIDENTS THAT ARE OF BLACK VOTING-AGE

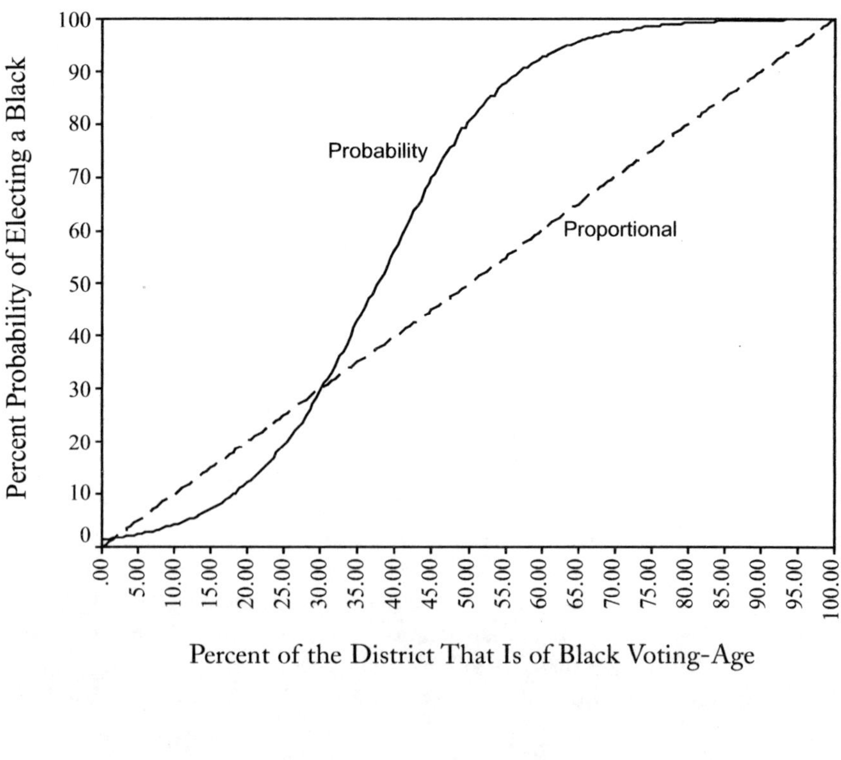

FIGURE 7.3

PERCENT BLACK POPULATION AND PERCENT DISTRICTED SEATS WITH BLACK REPRESENTATIVES BY ALL CITIES IN STUDY AND BY REGION

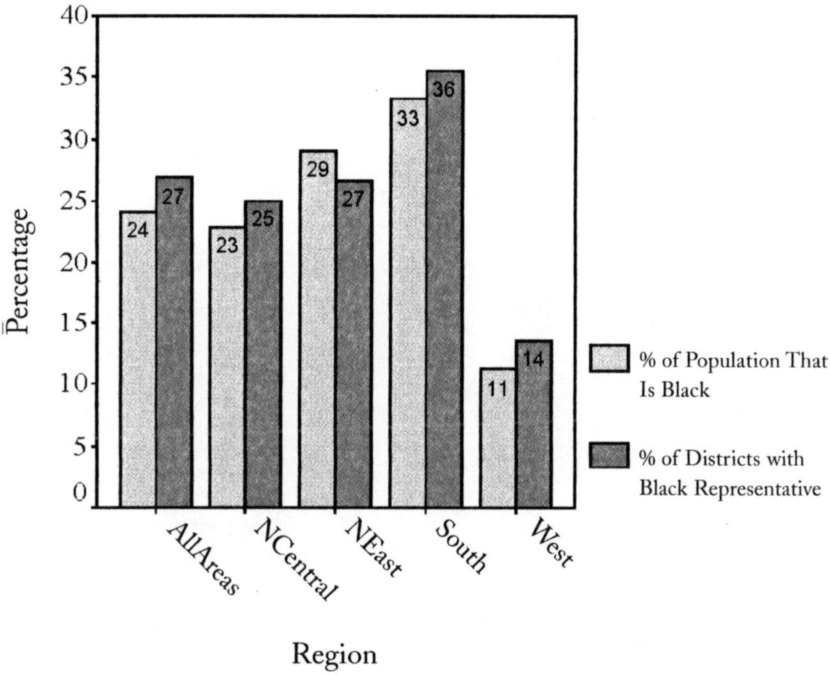

The size of the minority populations within our sample cities varies quite a bit, but within the total population of our sample cites there tends to be a higher percentage minority population relative to the national average (recall that we included cities with greater than 150,000 population, thus tapping many large urban areas). Figures 7.3 and 7.4 illustrate the percent of the entire population within our sample cities that is either black or Hispanic. In addition, these figures show the percent of all districted seats that have either black or Hispanic descriptive representatives. According to figure 7.3, 24 percent of the total population of our cities is black, yet black descriptive representatives occupy 27 percent of all districted seats. Simply, blacks tend to have a larger than proportionate share of council seats. This pattern holds true when our cities are aggregated by region, with the exception of the Northeast. In similar fashion, figure 7.4 shows that 17 percent of the total population within our cities is Hispanic, and Hispanic descriptive representatives occupy only 9 percent of all the districted seats. In general, Hispanics tend to be substantially underrepresented proportionate to their share of the population. While this pattern holds true across all the regions, there is much variation among regions. Within the north central region and Northeast, Hispanic underrepresentation is within a few percentage points. Within the South and West, however, there is substantial underrepresentation. Remarkably, within the West, Hispanics constitute 26 percent of the entire population, yet occupy only 15 percent of the districted seats.

FIGURE 7.4

PERCENT HISPANIC POPULATION AND PERCENT DISTRICTED SEATS WITH HISPANIC REPRESENTATIVES BY ALL CITIES IN STUDY AND BY REGION

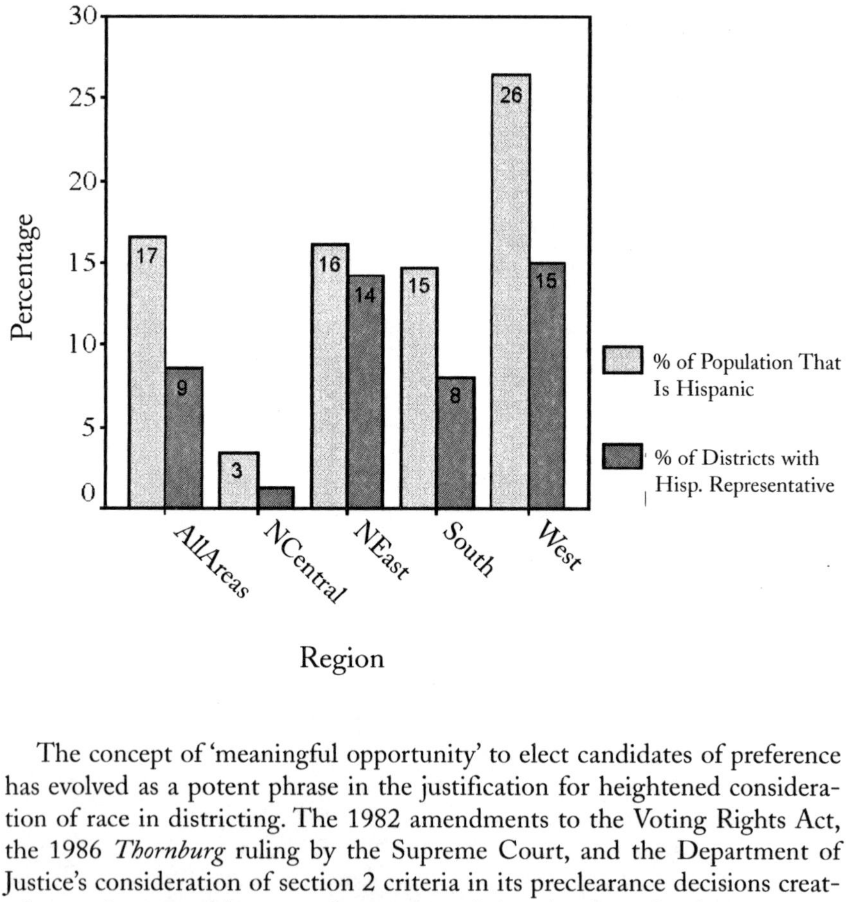

The concept of 'meaningful opportunity' to elect candidates of preference has evolved as a potent phrase in the justification for heightened consideration of race in districting. The 1982 amendments to the Voting Rights Act, the 1986 *Thornburg* ruling by the Supreme Court, and the Department of Justice's consideration of section 2 criteria in its preclearance decisions created an environment that strongly encouraged the adoption of majority-minority districts during the early 1990s. The adoption of many new majority-minority districts during the post-1990 round of redistricting has been credited with increases in minority descriptive representation. The size of the gains were most notable (and celebrated) at the national level, but gains also were made at the state level. The court rulings of *Shaw* (1993 and 1996)

and *Miller* (1995) rejected the erstwhile policy of encouraging jurisdictions to adopt additional majority-minority districts and stated that if race is predominant in the process, then strict scrutiny is applicable. The recent divided 5–4 court ruling of *Hunt v. Cromartie* (2001), revisiting North Carolina's twelfth congressional district redrawn following the *Shaw* rulings, upheld the plan as being motivated by political, rather than racial, considerations. May legislators now openly consider race if it is for political purposes? The ruling may be seen as the Court adjusting away from the post-1990 decisions that were read by many as labeling race strictly taboo.

There is far from a consensus on the impact these changes will have on the election of Hispanics and blacks in the coming decade. The criteria that guided city councils in redistricting efforts that began in April 2001 were ambiguous, providing latitude in decisions either to hold fast or to reduce the number of existing minority-opportunity districts. Some have dire predictions of what will come of the Court's evolving stance. Kousser (1999, 13, 16) states that the mid-1990s "reversal of the federal government's tenacious protection of minority voting rights . . . risks beginning again a process similar to that which unraveled the First Reconstruction" and that as many as half of all minority officials may be unseated in coming elections.

Many actors pressing for a greater priority being given to race are guided by the concept of 'racial fairness,' a notion critical to the evaluation of districting plans. The concept of fairness suggests that groups, either political or racial, should have an equal opportunity to register preferences and affect policy through the casting of ballots and election of representatives. The notion of group rights has been charged as offensive to the individual in that it assumes individual preferences are based on one's ascribed membership in a group. In regard to racial fairness, leveling the field of opportunity necessarily implies the consideration of race in the districting process under the assumption that the ethnicity or race of an individual behaves as a proxy for preference.

Hudson (1998, 3) argues that the federal courts' evolving interpretation of the Voting Rights Act has worked against the notions of "integration and assimilation" by emphasizing "polarity and separation." The Voting Rights Act was initially an instrument meant to codify the fifteenth Amendment and move blacks as group from exclusion to inclusion in the process of casting ballots. But the evolving judicial interpretations, and congressional amendments to the original act, have broadened the impact of the act to include not just simple access to the ballot box, but "meaningful inclusion" and "representation" by means of district manipulation (Bybee 1998, 19, 30). It has been argued that court intervention to thwart minority vote dilution is really intervention to prevent political defeat (e.g., Scarrow 2000).

Swain (1998, 195–96) suggests that the reasoning presented in recent court rulings will challenge "proponents of race-conscious districting to broaden their conceptualization of representation" and to recognize that a "substantial tradeoff exists between strategies that increase the substantive representation of African Americans and those that increase their descriptive representation." While the single-member district format may lead to increased black (or Hispanic) electoral success, this does not necessarily translate into opportunity to influence the legislative process (Guinier 1991a, 1991b, 1993, 1994).[2] Lublin (1997) argues that this is the central paradox of racial redistricting: majority-minority districts, while essential to the election of blacks and Hispanics, may result in a governing body less likely to be responsive to minority preferences (see also Cameron, Epstein, and O'Halloran 1996; Overby and Cosgrove 1996; Sullivan 1997, 106–07; Hudson 1998). The packing of "black voters and, for that matter, talented black candidates into ghettos" under the banner of increasing diversity in elected officials "carries heavy costs" (Voss and Lublin 2001, 145). While both Guinier generally and Lublin specifically are speaking to congressional districting, the same dilemma may appear at the municipal level (see also Viteritti 1994, 251–58).

The custom of turning over redistricting decisions to incumbent legislators may have contributed to a decline in competitive elections and, in turn, a decline in responsive representatives. An incumbent able to win with a margin above 10 percent may be considered to reside in a safe seat. The incentive to consider the policy preference of opposition constituents, whether defined by race or party, declines when reelection is certain. Competitive seats signal compromise and stimulate incumbents to be responsive to a greater diversity of interests within their districts due to the fact that coalition building becomes a necessary means to reelection. The idea of democracy and representation assumes a responsive relationship between the elected official and his constituents; unsecured seats that require coalition building, one may argue, are an effective electoral mechanism for a minority to achieve responsiveness through influence (see, e.g., Pildes 2002; Grose 2001). Perhaps the construction of districts with sizable minority populations not exceeding the 50 percent threshold, while far from guaranteeing the election of minority descriptive representatives, will make for more competitive elections, result in more responsiveness, and by extension, provide meaningful opportunity for minorities to have preferences considered in the policy process.

As long as elected legislators are instrumental in the development and adoption of districting plans it is safe to say that the courts will continue to play a prominent role in redistricting. It is unreasonable to expect elected officials performing the role of redistricters to be blind to the demographic and voting patterns of the city's residents. Race consciousness is ubiquitous. As one researcher put it, it is not possible to "impose ignorance" on redistricters (King, Bruce, and Gelman 1995, 90). It is also likely that the historic polarization in voting will continue, providing weight to arguments that race-conscious districting is a continuing necessity. In the context of these realities, we must expect the courts to continue to enter the thorny thicket of redistricting.

The future of Hispanic and black descriptive representation in this decade may be dependent on any number of variables. Some are subject to the winds of political fortune (or misfortune), and some are more predictable. It is clear that trends in minority population growth will continue to outpace that for whites, especially in many of the large urban areas. This is particularly true of the growing Hispanic populations in the South, West, and Northeast. U.S. Census projections indicate that the Hispanic population will surpass the black population by 2010.[3] These trends have the practical effect of increasing a minority's share of the potential voters within many single-member districts. In addition, some fear that the recent changes in the self-reporting options for race and ethnicity on the 2000 census could erode the potency of hard-won legal battles by not allowing social scientists and voting-rights activists to frame issues in austere white and black terms.

Also uncertain is how the evolving conservative partisanship at the state level will change the dynamics involved in redrawing districting plans that reduce, increase, or leave unchanged existing minority-opportunity districts at the local level. The trend in conservatism at the state level also may become evident at the local level in the near future, perhaps being witnessed first in the large cities. Currently twenty-nine states have Republican governors, and a majority of state legislatures are controlled by Republicans, markedly up from ten years ago. It has been argued that the packing of blacks into majority-minority districts may bleach the several surrounding districts, enhancing the ability of white Republican candidates to win. In contrast, it has been argued that Democrats in the South are unable to win elections in wholly white districts with, roughly, only one-third of nonblack voters identifying as Democrats. Democratic strategists have argued that districts with approximately 45 percent black population in conjunction with the remaining white Democrats provides the best opportunity to elect Democrats in many districts across the country.

Far less certain is the direction of the Supreme Court. Many of the recent Supreme Court decisions such as *Shaw* and *Cromartie* were decided by a Court with narrow 5–4 majorities. President Clinton's two appointees were supportive of the creation of majority-minority districts. It is a distinct possibility that Republican President George W. Bush will have the opportunity to appoint one or two, and perhaps three, new justices to the Supreme Court. Often attributed to have conservative tendencies, Chief Justice William H. Rehnquist, with over thirty years on the Court and in his late 70s, is a prime candidate for retirement since the election of Bush. Justice John Paul Stevens, a recent octogenarian, and Justice Sandra Day O'Conner, who just celebrated her seventieth birthday, also are candidates for retirement. Questions remain, too, about leadership at the Department of Justice and the vigor with which the Voting Rights Act will be prosecuted under the guidance of Attorney General John Ashcroft. As was seen in Ashcroft's confirmation process, as a precondition for confirmation many Democrats were looking for an affirmative statement in support of the "evolved" interpretations of the Voting Rights Act.

Much attention has been focused on the majority-minority single-member district as a vehicle to enhance the election opportunities of minority descriptive representatives. There is a strong theoretical expectation (and empirical evidence) that minority candidates will fare better in districts heavily populated with minorities. However, two important questions have received much less attention. First, provided that there is an available number of Hispanic or black residents in a city to theoretically construct minority-opportunity districts, why have such districts been adopted (and at what threshold level) in certain cities and not in others? Simply, under what conditions will municipalities adopt minority-opportunity districts? This research has answered this important question by first positing and then testing variables that condition this relationship. Second, the presence of districting plans with minority-opportunity districts does not necessarily assure the election of descriptive representatives. Why are minorities elected from some minority-opportunity districts and not others? Under what conditions do municipalities with minority-opportunity districts elect minorities and others not? This research has also shed light on this important question. This research has provided evidence suggesting that we ought to be cautions about applying to the local redistricting process districting assumptions made at the state level. Clearly, given the intimacy of politics and geography at the local level, inquiry into the dynamics of local districting merits much consideration.

Appendix A: Survey Design and Sample Questionnaires

Contacting cities consisted of a four-pronged approach that included phone, letter, fax, and electronic mail. It was clear that the survey questions concerning the race of past council members would most likely be answered by a person in either the city clerk's office or the mayor's office, while other questions concerning past litigation would best be directed to the city's law department. For fear that a comprehensive survey would decrease the response rate due to it being too time-consuming and burdensome for a single recipient, two separate surveys were initiated for each city. The process of surveying cities about either the race of past council members or past litigation began with initial phone inquiries to both the city council staff and the city attorney's office to identify the individuals most knowledgeable. Once these persons were identified and addresses confirmed, separate surveys were sent to each.

The survey process took place over a six-week period. The initial phone contacts occurred during the first week. The first wave of surveys, including cover letters, was faxed at the start of the second week. Recipients were encouraged to respond and return the information via fax. Frequently, as was the case in surveys sent to the cities' law departments, phone conversations were had to clarify the level of detail concerning litigation. Those not responding were sent a reminder note along with another copy of the survey at the beginning of week three. Those still not responding by the fourth week were sent via fax a reminder and another survey. In addition, the same reminder and survey were sent to the person via electronic mail. If a response was not received by the beginning of week five, a secondary contact person was identified and the survey mailed. If a response was not received from the secondary person by the beginning of week six, a reminder and another copy of the survey were sent via electronic mail (for timing between survey waves see Mangione 1995, 60–77).

Partial data on the type of election system (i.e., the number and type of election districts and the names of council members elected in the three elections following the city's redistricting) were obtained both from various national directories and official city web sites prior to the survey. Building on this partial data, each survey was tailored to each specific city depending on the amount of detail independently obtained. The following provides examples of typical survey letters sent to cities.

Department of Political Science **University of New Orleans**

303 Liberal Arts Building • New Orleans, LA 70148 •
Phone (504) XXX–XXXX • Fax (504) XXX–XXXX

PAGE 1 OF 2

TO: Mr. John Q. Smith, Clerk of Council
City of Anywhere
fax (330) XXX–XXXX

FM: Joshua G. Behr
University of New Orleans
Department of Political Science
fax (504) XXX–XXXX

Mr. Smith:

We are conducting a study of municipal elections systems. Among other items, we are interested in the race of recently elected council officials. We have listed below the names of officials elected to office in 1993, 1996, and 1999. Would you please, *to the best of your recollection*, identify the race of each official and fax these few pages back?

You may be assured that data on your city will be kept confidential. The results will not be associated with any specific individual. We will gladly send you the results of the entire study. Simply check the "Yes, send the results" box at the bottom of the last page.

Thank you in advance for your assistance. Should you have any questions about this project, please do not hesitate to contact me at (504) XXX–XXXX.

Persons in office in the year: **1999**						
Ward	**Councilperson**	***Please Circle***				
1	Horrigan	White	Black	Hispanic	Asian	Other
2	Mittiga	White	Black	Hispanic	Asian	Other
3	Sommerville	White	Black	Hispanic	Asian	Other
4	Greene	White	Black	Hispanic	Asian	Other
5	Shealey	White	Black	Hispanic	Asian	Other
6	Otterman	White	Black	Hispanic	Asian	Other
7	McAvoy	White	Black	Hispanic	Asian	Other
8	Keith	White	Black	Hispanic	Asian	Other

Persons in office in the year: **1996**						
Ward	**Councilperson**	***Please Circle***				
1	Bolden	White	Black	Hispanic	Asian	Other
2	Mendenhall	White	Black	Hispanic	Asian	Other
3	Sommerville	White	Black	Hispanic	Asian	Other
4	Williams	White	Black	Hispanic	Asian	Other
5	Tarle	White	Black	Hispanic	Asian	Other
6	Otterman	White	Black	Hispanic	Asian	Other
7	Bryant	White	Black	Hispanic	Asian	Other
8	Frank	White	Black	Hispanic	Asian	Other

Persons in office in the year: **1993**						
Ward	**Councilperson**	***Please Circle***				
1	Bolden	White	Black	Hispanic	Asian	Other
2	Mittiga	White	Black	Hispanic	Asian	Other
3	Sommerville	White	Black	Hispanic	Asian	Other
4	Williams	White	Black	Hispanic	Asian	Other
5	Tarle	White	Black	Hispanic	Asian	Other
6	Otterman	White	Black	Hispanic	Asian	Other
7	Bryant	White	Black	Hispanic	Asian	Other
8	Frank	White	Black	Hispanic	Asian	Other

Thank you!

Please fax back to: (504) XXX–XXXX

☐ "Yes, please send me the results of the study."
(Check the box)

Department of Political Science ______________ **University of New Orleans**

303 Liberal Arts Building • New Orleans, LA 70148 •
Phone (504) XXX–XXXX • Fax (504) XXX–XXXX

PAGE 1 OF 1

TO: Mr. John Q. Smith, Clerk of Council
City of Anywhere
fax (402) XXX–XXXX

FM: Joshua G. Behr
University of New Orleans
Department of Political Science
phone (504) XXX–XXXX

John,

We are conducting a study of municipal election systems. Among other items, we are interested in the occurrence of voting rights litigation. Will you please, ***to the best of your recollection***, answer the following question:

> **Was the city engaged in any form of voting rights litigation between the 1980 and 1990 rounds of redistricting of the city's council districts?**
>
> **At this point we don't need to know any details concerning the litigation—just need to know if there was litigation or not.**

☐ YES ☐ NO

You may be assured that data on your city will be kept confidential. The results will not be associated with any specific individual. We will gladly send you the results of the entire study.

Thank you for your assistance. Should you have any questions about this project, please do not hesitate to contact me at (504) XXX–XXXX.

Thank you!

Please fax back to: (504) XXX–XXXX

☐ "Yes, please send me the results of the study."
(Check the box)

Appendix B: Cities Surveyed

Akron, Ohio	Corpus Christi, Tex.	Indianapolis, Ind.
Albuquerque, N. Mex.	Dallas, Tex.	Inglewood, Calif.
Anchorage, Ark.	Denver, Colo.	Jackson, Miss.
Arlington, Tex.	Des Moines, Iowa	Jacksonville, Fla.
Atlanta, Ga.	District of Columbia	Jersey City, N.J.
Aurora, Colo.	Durham, N.C.	Kansas City, Kans.
Bakersfield, Calif.	El Paso, Tex.	Kansas City, Mo.
Baltimore, Md.	Elizabeth, N.J.	Knoxville, Tenn.
Baton Rouge, La.	Flint, Mich.	Lansing, Mich.
Beaumont, Tex.	Fort Lauderdale, Fla.	Laredo, Tex.
Birmingham, Ala.	Fort Wayne, Ind.	Las Vegas, Nev.
Boston, Mass.	Fort Worth, Tex.	Lexington-Fayette, Ky.
Bridgeport, Conn.	Fresno, Calif.	Lincoln, Neb.
Buffalo, N.Y.	Glendale, Ariz.	Little Rock, Ark.
Charlotte, N.C.	Grand Rapids, Mich.	Long Beach, Calif.
Chattanooga, Tenn.	Greensboro, N.C.	Los Angeles, Calif.
Cleveland, Ohio	Honolulu, Hawaii	Louisville, Ky.
Colorado Springs, Colo.	Houston, Tex.	Lubbock, Tex.
Columbus, Ga.	Huntsville, Ala.	Madison, Wis.

Memphis, Tenn.	Philadelphia, Penn.	San Bernardino, Calif.
Miami, Fla.	Phoenix, Ariz.	San Diego, Calif.
Milwaukee, Wis.	Pittsburgh, Penn.	San Jose, Calif.
Minneapolis, Minn.	Pomona, Calif.	Savannah, Ga.
Mobile, Ala.	Providence, R.I.	Shreveport, La.
Montgomery, Ala.	Raleigh, N.C.	South Bend, Ind.
Moreno Valley, Calif.	Reno, Nev.	Springfield, Ill.
New Haven, Conn.	Richmond, Va.	Stockton, Calif.
New Orleans, La.	Riverside, Calif.	Syracuse, N.Y.
Newark, N.J.	Rochester, N.Y.	Tacoma, Wash.
Norfolk, Va.	Rockford, Ill.	Tampa, Fla.
Oakland, Calif.	Sacramento, Calif.	Toledo, Ohio
Oklahoma City, Okla.	Saint Louis, Mo.	Tucson, Ariz.
Omaha, Neb.	Saint Paul, Minn.	Tulsa, Okla.
Orlando, Fla.	Saint Petersburg, Fla.	Virginia Beach, Va.
Pasadena, Calif.	Salinas, Calif.	Wichita, Kans.
Pasadena, Tex.	Salt Lake City, Utah	Winston-Salem, N.C.
Paterson, N.J.	San Antonio, Tex.	Worcester, Mass.

Appendix C: Cases Cited

Allen v. State Board of Elections 393 U.S. 544 (1969)

Arlington Heights v. Metropolitan Housing Development Corp. 429 U.S. 252 (1977)

Avery v. Midland County 390 U.S. 474 (1968)

Barnett v. City of Chicago 97–2792 (7th Cir. Ct. of Appeals. 1998)

Beer v. United States 425 U.S. 130 (1976)

Brown and United States v. Board of School Commissioners of Mobile County 466 U.S. 1005 (1983)

Bush v. Vera 517 U.S. 952 (1996)

City of Lockhart v. United States 460 U.S. 125 (1983)

City of Mobile v. Bolden 446 U.S. 55 (1980), *rem'd Brown and United States v. Board of School Commissioners of Mobile County* 542 F. Supp. 1078 (S.D. Ala. 1982), *aff'd* 706 F.2d 1103 (11th Cir. Ct. of Appeals 1983), *aff'd* 464 U.S. 1005 (1983)

Forston v. Dorsey 379 U.S. 433 (1965)

Garza v. Los Angeles County Board of Supervisors 918 F.2d (9th Cir. Ct. of Appeals 1990)

Gray v. Sanders 372 U.S. 368 (1963)

Growe v. Emison 507 U.S. 25 (1993)

Hayes v. Louisiana (1993)

Holder v. Hall 512 U.S. 874 (1994)

Hunt v. Cromartie 526 U.S. 541 (2001)

Jeffers v. Clinton 730 F.Supp. 196 (E.D. Ark. 1989)

Johnson v. DeGrandy 512 U.S. 997 (1994)

Ketchum v. Byrne 740 F.2d 1398 (7th Cir. Ct. of Appeals 1984)

Kirksey v. Board of Supervisors of Hinds County, Mississippi 554 F.2d 139 (1977)

Miller v. Johnson 515 U.S. 900 (1995)

Presley v. Etowah County Commission 502 U.S. 491 (1992)

Reno v. Bossier Parish School Board 120 U.S. 866 (2000)

Reynolds v. Sims 377 U.S. 533 (1964)

Rogers v. Lodge 458 U.S. 613 (1982)

Shaw v. Hunt 517 U.S. 899 (1996)

Shaw v. Reno 509 U.S. 630 (1993)

Thornburg v. Gingles 478 U.S. 30 (1986)

United Jewish Organizations v. Carey 430 U.S. 144 (1977)

Whitcomb v. Chavis 403 U.S. 124 (1971)

White v. Regester 412 U.S. 755 (1973)

Wise v. Lipscomb 437 U.S. 535 (1978)

Zimmer v. McKeithen 485 F.2d 1297 (5th Cir. Ct. of Appeals 1973)

Appendix D: Operational Definition of Region

WEST	NORTH CENTRAL	SOUTH	NORTHEAST
Alaska	North Dakota	Arkansas	Pennsylvania
Washington	South Dakota	Texas	New York
Oregon	Minnesota	Louisiana	New Jersey
California	Iowa	Mississippi	Connecticut
Hawaii	Nebraska	Tennessee	Rhode Island
Montana	Kansas	Kentucky	Massachusetts
Idaho	Missouri	Alabama	New Hampshire
Nevada	Wisconsin	Georgia	Vermont
Wyoming	Illinois	Florida	Maine
Utah	Michigan	South Carolina	
Colorado	Indiana	North Carolina	
Arizona	Ohio	Virginia	
New Mexico	Oklahoma	West Virginia	
		Maryland	
		District of Columbia	
		Delaware	

Notes

Chapter One

1. With the right to cast ballots secure, most voting-rights advocates have advanced the single-member district election format as the preferred remedy for minority vote dilution under the at-large format (Barker 1994). For the limitations of the single-member district as a remedy for the dilution of the voting strength of several minority groups in multiethnic cities, see Reed (1993), Macchiarola and Diaz (1993a, 1993b, 1993c), and Mollenkopf, Olson, and Ross (2001, 51–62).

2. Sloan 1969; Campbell and Feagin 1975; Karnig 1976; Jones 1976, 1979; Robinson and Dye 1978; Taebel 1978; Davidson 1979; Latimer 1979; Berry and Dye 1979, especially 113–22; Karnig and Welch 1980, 79–83, 1982; Davidson and Korbell 1981, 992–98; Vedlitz and Johnson 1982, 733–34; Mundt and Heilig 1982, 1046; Heilig and Mundt 1984, 62–64; Engstrom and McDonald 1981, 1982, 1986, 1987; Ball 1986, 30–33; Teasley 1987; Brouthers and Larson 1988; Welch 1990; McDonald and Engstrom 1992; Moncrief and Thompson 1992; Burton et al. 1994, 217–25; Renner 1999; Walawender 1999; for county level see Bullock 1994; Burton et al. 1994; McDonald et al. 1994; Keech and Sistrom 1994; Sass and Mehay 1995; for school boards see Stewart, England, and Meier 1989; Hill and Redix-Smalls 2002; for a discussion of SMDs enhancing the election of a *white* minority see Haeberle 1997, 287–89.

3. Gay (2001) finds that the election to Congress of a black descriptive representative may decrease the voting participation of whites while only slightly increasing the voting participation of blacks.

4. Parent and Stekler (1985, 221) note that the black community may not be homogeneous; class stratification within the black community raises the potential for political divisions (see also Canon, Schousen, and Sellers 1996, especially 849–50; Johnson 2002, 131–35).

5. The city council in some cities is elected by a combination of both at-large designated seats and single-member district designated seats. Thus, a "mixed" format.

6. See, for example, Brace et al. 1988; Grofman and Handley 1989b; Grofman, Handley, and Niemi 1992, 118; Hudson 1998, 153–54; *Kirksey v. Board of Supervisors of Hinds County, Mississippi*, 554 F.2d 139, 1977; *United Jewish Organizations of Williamsburgh v. Carey*, 430 U.S. 144, 1977; *Ketchum v. Byrne* 740 F.2d 1398 7th Cir. Ct. of Appeals, 1984; *Barnett v. City of Chicago* 97–2792 7th Cir. Ct. of Appeals, 1998.

CHAPTER TWO

1. The presence of blacks on governing bodies at the local level is higher in the South than elsewhere. This is explained by the regional difference in the percentage of cities that have substantial black populations. Among nonsouthern cities with at least 10 percent black population, about 8 percent have a black population above 40 percent. This contrasts with the South, where 20 percent of such cities exceed 40 percent black population (Grofman and Handley 1989a, 272–74). The assumption is that a larger black population is conducive to the election of black candidates. Substantially more southern cities with a minimum threshold of blacks have a black population large enough to elect candidates of choice.

2. By adjusting the number of councilmanic seats within a single-member district system, a threshold of exclusion can be manipulated to exclude smaller groups (Engstrom 1987). The threshold of exclusion is the minimum percentage of the electorate that a group must constitute in order to have a numeric opportunity to elect a candidate of choice, given the "worst case" assumptions about the behavior of the other voters. In this case a six-seat council excludes all groups that constitute 10 percent or less of the entire citywide population.

CHAPTER THREE

1. Rogerson and Yang (1999, 27) suggest that the identification of a city's maximal number of majority-minority districts is an "analytical" matter divorced from the more "complex" problems of urban geography.

2. It has been argued that *Shaw* and its progeny steer away from embracing proportional representation for protected minorities that are spatially dispersed among nonminorities yet allow for race-conscious districting when minorities "live in distinct, easily identifiable clusters" (Forest 1995, esp. 104–05).

3. Massey and Denton (1988b) argue that segregation is a multidimensional phenomenon that includes five conceptually distinct facets. The relative eveness of a group's distribution throughout the city may provide for the group being overrepresented in some areas and underrepresented in others. Or perhaps the group may be concentrated residentially in smaller geographic spaces than another group. The group may be more centralized around a city core or may be clustered to form an enclave. Last, the exposure of a group to other groups may be conditioned by the number of neighborhoods that are shared by multiple groups. As explained by Massey and Denton (1988b, 283), "a group that is highly centralized, spatially concentrated, unevenly distributed, tightly clustered, and minimally exposed to majority members is said to be residentially 'segregated.' Although the five dimensions overlap empirically—a group segregated on one dimension also tends to be segregated on another—they are conceptually distinct" (see also Harrison and Weinberg 1992). Of these five dimensions of the concept segregation, evenness fits my theoretical concerns the best. Evenness is employed to tap the concept of political tenability and is discussed more fully in the methods section.

4. The increased number of districts and the consequent smaller district population size means that a significant percentage of the minority community (nearly 36 percent in the seven-seat example) may potentially be placed outside the minority-opportunity district, and therefore the "influence" of the minority in the electorate may

extend well beyond the one minority-opportunity district. According to Grofman et al. (1982, 21), "minority representation might actually be increased not by raising the number of black office holders but by increasing the number of office holders, black and white, who have to appeal to the blacks to win." While minority "influence" is important, this research is focused more narrowly to provide an explanation of the construction of minority-opportunity districts and the minority presence on the governing body. Discussion of influence districts is visited in chapter 7.

5. A single seat on a five-, seven-, or nine-member council may wield substantial influence, especially as the swing vote in the creation of a majority coalition, and therefore is likely to stimulate local political opposition to the creation of a minority-opportunity district. The acquisition of one seat on a five- or seven-member council may be perceived as a serious threat to the hegemony of whites (e.g., Karnig and Welch 1980, 28; Taebel 1978, 51). But on a relatively large council, say twelve or fifteen members, the presence of a single black member is not likely to be as threatening (Davidson 1984, 7). Indeed, the presence of the minority seat may reassure the white power structure that its city is "racially progressive." Concession of a single seat may be a "symbolic gesture" by the dominant majority (Alozie and Manganaro 1993, 295).

6. Even cities with widely divergent population sizes tend to have small councils.

7. Differences have been illustrated between black, Hispanic, and Asian representation associated with type of election system (Taebel 1978, 145–46; Lyons and Jewell 1988, 441–42; Tobin 1987; Welch 1990; Zax 1990; Bullock and MacManus 1990; Polinard, Wrinkle, and Longoria 1991; Harrison and Weinberg 1992; Engstrom and McDonald 1986; McDonald and Engstrom 1992, 130–39; Alozie 1993; Brischetto 1998, 57–59). For a discussion of the competing districting claims that arise when minority groups are geographically commingled, see Reed 1992, esp. 769–70, Grofman and Handley 1989b, and Clark and Morrison 1995.

8. It has been shown that Hispanics and Asians have higher levels of residential integration than blacks (Boal 1976, 59–61; Lopez 1981; Macchiarola and Diaz 1993a, 211–13, 1993b, 1200–01, 1207; Reed 1993, 770, 776 note 74; Hardy-Fanta 1993, 112–14; Denton and Massey 1988; Massey 1979, 1988, 1994; Massey, Gross, and Eggers 1991; Massey and Denton 1987, 1988a, 1988b, 1989, 1993, esp. 20–33, 61–70, 85; Massey and Hajnal 1995; Henry 1994, 22; Adams 2000, 31 and 230; Charles 2001, 271–89; Meyer 2000, esp. 212–14; for a discussion of the differences in segregation for black Hispanics and white Hispanics see Rosenbaum 1996).

9. The responsibility for adopting councilmanic districts is usually placed with the city council (*Wise v. Lipscomb* 437 U.S. 535, 1978; Strange 1989).

10. Incumbency is the best determinant of election, in spite of the candidate's race or policy preferences (for general discussion see Flanigan and Zingale 1998, 183–88).

11. According to Gelman and King (1994), during the redistricting process an incumbent must strike a balance between the individual interest of maximizing the probability of his reelection and the larger interest of maintaining or increasing his party's share of seats. An increase in the probability of individual reelection may be at the expense of the current partisan balance. I assert that there is a similar tension between a minority incumbent's desire for reelection and his desire to increase the probability of the election of additional members of his group.

12. The process of redistricting in the United States is so contentious that disputes arising at the start of a decade often are not settled fully and are "often made obsolete by the beginning of a new round of redistricting" (Kubin 1997, 837; Issacharoff and Pildes 1996, 25; Eagles, Katz, and Mark 1999; Charles and Roberts 2001, 10–11; Webster 2002, 118). Even an "independent" boundary commission charged with districting, such as that used in Britain, will construct districts that will favor one political or racial group and disadvantage others. Even if a group's resultant electoral advantage was unintentional, charges of commission bias will surely arise (Lakeman 1974, 46; Lyons 1969; Rossiter, Johnston, and Pattic 1997). But, as Monmonier (2001, 99–103) notes, although not totally neutral, independent redistricting commissions, with legislative bodies setting the criteria, present an attractive alternative to legislative dominance in the process. In the 2000 round of redistricting the states of Washington and Iowa turned over the drawing of boundaries to independent or nonpartisan commissions.

13. 79 Stat. 437, as amended by the Civil Rights Act of 1968, 82 Stat. 73, the Voting Rights Act Amendments of 1970, 84 Stat. 314, the District of Columbia Delegate Act, 84 Stat. 853, the Voting Rights Act Amendments of 1975, 89 Stat. 400, the Voting Rights Act Amendments of 1982, 96 Stat. 131, and the Voting Rights Language Assistance Act of 1992, Public Law 102–344, 106 Stat. 921, 42 U.S.C. 1973 et seq.

14. The potential of the preclearance provisions to be used by the Department of Justice to scrutinize not only changes in state and local procedures concerning the casting of ballots but also the way in which electoral competition is structured was not immediately realized. But by 1969 the Supreme Court had accepted a broad, inclusive interpretation of what qualified as a "voting qualification or prerequisite to voting, or standard, practice or procedure" (see *Allen v. State Board of Elections* 1969). Fewer than two hundred changes had been submitted through 1968, but submissions increased rapidly during the 1970s (Engstrom 1994, 687). Since 1965 several hundred thousand changes in electoral laws or procedures have been submitted for approval under the preclearance provisions, and less than 2 percent have met with Department of Justice objections (see O'Rourke 1992, esp. 86–87; see also Posner 1996, 88–90; Foster 1986).

15. Section 2(a) read, in part, "No voting qualification or prerequisite to voting, or standard, practice, or procedure shall be imposed or applied by any state or political subdivision to deny or abridge the right of any citizen" to vote.

16. The Court had earlier found malapportionment an unconstitutional form of vote dilution at both the state and local levels (see, e.g., *Gray v. Sanders* 1963, *Reynolds v. Sims* 1964, *Avery v. Midland County* 1968). But by 1965, in *Forston v. Dorsey*, the Court recognized that multi-member districts that had the effect, whether intentional or not, of canceling-out minority voting strength may be potentially unconstitutional. In *Whitcomb v. Chavis* (1971) the Supreme Court, in reversing a district court's finding of unconstitutional vote dilution in a multimember system, stated that the mere absence of minority descriptive representation alone does not demonstrate dilution; additional evidence demonstrating less opportunity would be necessary to sustain a fourteenth Amendment claim. In *White v. Register* (1973), another challenge to multi-member districts, the Supreme Court upheld for the first time a district court finding of dilution on the grounds that a totality of circumstances demonstrated that minorities had less opportunity to participate in politics and elect candidates of choice.

In upholding the lower court finding, though, the Supreme Court failed to provide any further specificity as to the relative importance of the individual circumstances. The Court, however, made clear that discriminatory *effect* was acceptable proof of dilution; discriminatory *intent* would not be required.

17. In *Zimmer*, issued within months of the *White* decision, the fifth Circuit Court of Appeals distilled further the circumstances cited in *White* by instructing the federal district courts to consider eight criteria, four primary and four enhancing, as relevant in a dilution claim. Over the next eight years numerous multimember schemes within Louisiana were ruled dilutive based on the *Zimmer* criteria (Engstrom et al. 1994, 117).

18. The burden placed on plaintiffs to show an election system to be dilutive was still great following *Zimmer*. While the *Zimmer* decision culled circumstances to eight factors, these covered tremendous ground; plaintiffs, to be safe, would often compile detailed historical records of race relations within the challenged jurisdiction (see Davidson 1994, 28–29).

19. Mobile's at-large commission form of government was adopted in 1911. According to the Court's 1980 *Bolden* intent standard, in order to establish a violation of the fourteenth Amendment's Equal Protection Clause plaintiffs were faced with the daunting task of uncovering what was tantamount to a smoking gun. The Court had remanded the case to the district court stating that a factual finding of intent to dilute by the city leaders at the time the plan was adopted would be necessary to demonstrate a fourteenth Amendment violation. According to Davidson (1994, 34), the enunciated intent standard appeared "to be the straw that would break the camel's back in voting rights cases, where the load borne by the plaintiffs' camel was already heavy. It was not simply one more burden equal in importance to the eight other *Zimmer* factors." On remand, however, plaintiffs, along with the Department of Justice (acting as an intervenor), produced exhaustive testimony from historians and expert witnesses demonstrating that the format was indeed adopted with discriminatory purpose. The Supreme Court affirmed that intent had now been demonstrated and upheld the lower courts' findings that the at-large system violated the fourteenth Amendment (*Brown and United States v. Board of School Commissioners of Mobile County* , 542 F. Supp. 1078 (S.D. Ala. 1982), *aff'd* 706 F.2d 1103 (11th Cir. Ct. of Appeals 1983), *aff'd* 464 U.S. 1005 (1983)).

20. The Supreme Court's ruling in *Bolden* ratched-up the bar necessary for plaintiffs to demonstrate vote dilution under the fourteenth Amendment. The section 2 amendment was intended to provide "a general statutory protection against dilutive schemes" and restore the *White-Zimmer* standard (Engstrom et al. 1994, 117; see also Davis 1995, 313–14).

21. Civil rights groups pressed hard for the addition of the "results standard" to section 2 (Thernstrom 1987). Many in Congress had resisted the proposed amendment fearing that such a standard would lead to a proportional representation mandate. To mitigate these concerns compromise language was pushed by Senator Robert Dole of Kansas. Section 2(b) was amended, in part, to read: "the extent to which members of a protected class have been elected . . . is one circumstance which may be considered: *Provided*, that nothing in this section establishes a right to have members of a protected class elected in numbers equal to their proportion in the population." This language was meant to assuage the fears that a legal entitlement to a given level

of electoral success would be established (see, e.g., Bullock 1999, 216–17; Teasley 1987, 96–97; Issacharoff, Karlan, and Pildes 1998, 419–24; Pildes 1997, 2518–23; Blumstein 1995, 566–69; Parker 1983, 748–51).

22. An increase in litigation in areas not covered by the preclearance provisions followed the 1982 amendments as section 2 became an important tool to challenge election systems as dilutive to minority voting strength (for a general discussion of the increase in litigation challenging 1990 redistrictings, see Weber 1995).

23. Interestingly, several days following the signing of the 1982 amendments by President Ronald Reagan the Supreme Court tempered its *Bolden* intent standard in another fourteenth Amendment vote dilution case involving an at-large system, *Rogers v. Lodge* (1981). In *Rogers*, as in *Bolden*, the Court required plaintiffs to demonstrate intent. But unlike *Bolden*, the Court reasoned that a totality of relevant circumstantial factors similar to the *Zimmer* criteria may be used to *infer* intent in a fourteenth Amendment vote dilution claim. The Court's apparent reversal has been attributed to both a change in the composition of the Court and the Court's awareness of the vocal criticism of the *Bolden* ruling from voting-rights advocates and Congress alike (see, e.g., McDonald 1992, 68–69).

24. Although *Thornburg* addressed dilution in multimember formats, the *Gingles* test was assumed widely to apply to the single-member district context as well. Later, in *Growe v. Emison* (1993), the Court indeed stated that the same standards that apply in multimember formats to establish a section 2 claim of vote dilution also applied to single-member district formats. In *Johnson v. DeGrandy* (512 U.S. 997 at 1246 (1994)) the Court confirmed that "the *Gingles* factors are merely *pre-conditions* which are not necessarily enough by themselves to require judicial relief"; the additional circumstances listed in *Gingles*, and possibly others, should be considered, in their totality, to support evidence of dilution (McKaskle 1995, 6 n18).

25. The argument is well made that this assertion is mistaken (see, e.g., Dunne 1993; Posner 1996, 95–110; Grofman and Handley 1996, 72 n16). Savage (1995, 24) notes that while there was not an explicit maximization policy the Department of Justice's application of the preclearance mechanism influenced the districting process "by *prodding* states to create as many black majority districts as possible" (emphasis added).

26. McKaskle (1995) argues that post 1990 redistricters were "pragmatic" in their desire to avoid potential litigation. The 1982 amendments to section 2 and subsequent rulings presented redistricters with two seemingly contradictory cues. First, districting plans should provide minorities with the opportunity to elect candidates of choice. Second, this does not require that plans insure the proportional representation of minorities. According to McKaskel, districters were disinclined to propose bizarre districts that were based solely on race. But in preclearance jurisdictions that met the first prong of the three-prong *Gingles* test (minority is sufficiently numerous and geographically compact), the redistricters were pragmatic. Even if polarized voting, the second and third prongs of the *Gingles* test, was not clearly evident the desire to avoid potential litigation prompted the proposal of majority-minority districts. According to Grofman and Handley (1996, 77 n5), "By anticipating how courts and DOJ will interpret the Act, legislators frequently make changes they would not otherwise have made to reduce the likelihood of a plan being overturned." see also Peterson 1995, 10–11; Webster 2000, 148.

27. Organizations concerned with minority voting rights (e.g., Center for Constitutional Rights, NAACP Legal Defense and Education Fund, Southern Regional Council, Southern Poverty Law Center, American Civil Liberties Union, League of United Latin American Citizens, Latino Political Action Committee, Lawyers' Committee for Civil Rights Under Law, Southwest Voter Research Institute, National Voting Rights Institute, Georgia Legal Services, Mexican-American Legal Defense and Education Fund, Puerto Rican Legal Defense and Education Fund, Asian-American Legal Defense and Education Fund) may scrutinize municipal districting plans, especially those in covered jurisdictions. (For a discussion of the NAACP in litigation, see Burton et al. 1994, 211–12; for a discussion of MALDEF in litigation, see Chavez 1992, 82–85).

28. Although the ultimate power to write and amend the Code of Federal Regulations (CFR) rests with Congress, the attorney general, in practice, may propose specific regulatory language during the congressional rulemaking process. The federal courts defer to the attorney general's interpretation of the Voting Rights Act generally, and the administration of section 5 specifically, especially on matters to which Congress has not expressed an opinion (see, e.g., *Presley v. Etowah County Commission* 1992; Ball, Krane, and Lauth 1982).

29. Covered jurisdictions must, upon submission of the proposed change for administrative approval, demonstrate that "the opportunity for the public to be heard, and of the opportunity for interested parties to participate in the decision to adopt the proposed change . . . especially by minority group members, in fact took place" (28 CFR 51.28(f)). The efforts of covered jurisdictions to include the participation of language minorities prior to submission of the proposed changes will be considered a relevant factor by the attorney general in his decision to approve a plan: covered jurisdictions, for example, must make an effort to "afford members of racial and language minority groups an opportunity to participate in the decision to make the [proposed] change" (28 CFR 51.57(c)). Further, complaints may be registered with the Department of Justice. In theory, the opening of the districting process to the public through hearings or the solicitation of input from interested parties provides the opportunity for minority communities to be heard at least, although some may argue that this requirement in fact may be mere formality with districting decisions made behind closed doors (see, e.g., Scher, Mills, and Hotaling 1997, 265–66).

30. The Supreme Court has since responded to discordant lower court rulings by providing an ordering of race-related criteria relative to race-neutral criteria. The Court has stated that if traditional districting principles are subordinated to race in the districting process (i.e., race is used as the predominant factor), then this triggers "strict scrutiny" because any racial classification is inherently suspect. In order for a proposed change to satisfy strict scrutiny a state or municipality that uses race as a predominant criterion must have both a "compelling interest" in doing so and present a plan tailored "narrowly" to further that compelling interest (see *Shaw v. Reno* 1993, *Shaw v. Hunt* 1996, *Miller v. Johnson* 1995, *Hunt v. Comartie* 2001).

31. For example, Engstrom and McDonald (1986, 1987) find that a reduction in resource disparity contributes to a reduction in black under-representation and that this reduction is greater in the South than the non-South.

CHAPTER FOUR

1. Due to unresponsiveness, the data for New York City and Chicago are not included. In addition, these cities have unusually large councils (fifty single-member districts in each) relative to other cities in the study.

2. Various sources were used to increase the response rate of surveys or to confirm the accuracy of collected data through cross references. These sources include the Municipal Yellow Book, Carrol's Municipal/County Directory, National Roster of Hispanic Elected Officials, Roster of Black Elected Officials, and the Directory of City Policy Officials.

3. The index has been used over a period of decades, for example, to measure the dissimilarity between a central urban area and its suburbs to illustrate the flight of whites from urban centers (see, e.g., Massey and Denton 1993).

CHAPTER 5

1. The assumption of a simple additive multiple regression model is that the effect of each independent variable on the dependent variable is the same across all cities, regardless of the level of the other independent variables. However, in this analysis each specifying variable interacts with system aptitude to produce a multiplicative interaction term. Therefore, the effect of system aptitude on the dependent variable is contingent on the value of the specifying variable (see Friedrich 1982).

2. This pattern of lower levels of segregation for Hispanic cities relative to black cities remains when cities are disaggregated by region. For the nine Hispanic cities in the Northeast the mean segregation score is .458 (Std. Dev. .092), while for the eleven black cities in the Northeast the mean segregation score is .659 (Std. Dev. .081). For the ten Hispanic cities in the South the mean segregation score is .599 (Std. Dev. .113), while for the forty-one black cities in that region the mean segregation score is .736 (Std. Dev. .078). For the twenty-three Hispanic cities in the West the mean segregation score is .466 (Std. Dev. .116), while for the fifteen black cities in that region the mean segregation score is .526 (Std. Dev. .129). In the north central region there are just two cities in the Hispanic category, Cleveland with a segregation score of .645, and Milwaukee with a segregation score of .595, yielding a mean of .618, and nineteen black cities in this region with a mean segregation score of .701 (Std. Dev. .100). For the identification of regions, see appendix D.

3. The R^2 presented in table 5.3 provides a measure of how much of the variance in the dependent variable is accounted for by the *single* independent variable, system aptitude. The adjusted R^2 presented in table 5.4 concerns the variance accounted for by *several* independent variables.

4. Notice that in this case (Hispanics at the 60 percent threshold) the adjusted intercepts are quite low, from -.088 to -.275, and the range between the two is about 19 percentage points. Also the range between the reported slope coefficients is 12.9 percentage points. These magnitudes in ranges are not found at either the 55 or 50 percent thresholds (10.1 and 10.0 percentage points for the slope coefficients and .3 and 3.5 percentage points for the intercepts, respectively). This suggests that the impact of vested advocacy at the 60 percent threshold is more pronounced relative to the impact at either the 55 or 50 percent threshold.

CHAPTER 6

1. It is evident that there are many instances where districted Hispanic or black officials are elected from districts with respective minority populations below the minimum 50 percent minority voting-age population threshold established in this research. In fact, there are cities that do not have the theoretical aptitude to create a single minority-opportunity district, yet have elected districted Hispanic and black officials. An analysis in the following chapter examines these cases.

2. This pattern of lower levels of resource disparity for Hispanic cities relative to black cities varies when cities are disaggregated by region. For the five Hispanic cities in the Northeast the mean resource disparity score is .354 (Std. Dev. .139), while for the six black cities in the Northeast the mean resource disparity score is .356 (Std. Dev. .077). For the nine Hispanic cities in the South the mean resource disparity score is .457 (Std. Dev .178), while for the thirty-seven black cities in that region the mean resource disparity score is .563 (Std. Dev. .080). For the eleven Hispanic cities in the West the mean resource disparity score is .491 (Std. Dev. .126), while for the three black cities in that region the mean resource disparity score is .308 (Std. Dev. .356). In the North Central region there are no Hispanic cities in the analysis, while the fourteen black cities in this region have a mean resource disparity score of .445 (Std. Dev. .079). For the identification of regions, see appendix D.

CHAPTER 7

1. Binary logistic regressions are run with the dependent dichotomous variable being either the presence or absence of a minority official, either Hispanic or black. The covariate, or independent variable, is the proportion of the district that is voting-age, either Hispanic or black. The predicted probabilities from these analyses are plotted and presented below.

2. Guinier advocates in some instances, in lieu of the single-member district format, the use of the at-large, cumulative voting election system (for an introduction to Guinier's arguments, see Kennedy 1995).

3. For U.S. Census Bureau projections see www.census.gov/population/projections/popproj.

Bibliography

Adams, Florence. 2000. *Latinos and Local Representation: Changing Realities, Emerging Theories.* New York: Garland.

Allen, James P., and Eugene Turner. 1995. "Ethnic Differentiation by Blocks within Census Tracts." *Urban Geography* 16 (April):344–64.

Alozie, Nicholas O. 1992. "The Election of Asians to City Councils." *Social Science Quarterly* 77 (March):90–100.

Alozie, Nicholas O., and Lynne L. Manganaro. 1993. "Black and Hispanic Council Representation: Does Council Size Matter?" *Urban Affairs Quarterly* 29 (December):276–95.

Ayres, Q. Whitfield, and David Whiteman. 1984. "Congressional Reapportionment in the 1980s: Types and Determinants of Policy Outcomes." *Political Science Quarterly* 99 (Summer):303–14.

Ball, Howard. 1986. "Racial Vote Dilution: Impact of the Reagan DOJ and the Burger Court on the Voting Rights Act." *Publius* 16 (Winter):29–48.

Ball, Howard, Dale Krane, and Thomas P. Lauth. 1982. *Compromised Compliance: The Implementation of the 1965 Voting Rights Act.* Westport: Greenwood.

Banfield, Edward C., and James Q. Wilson. 1963. *City Politics.* New York: Vintage.

Barker, Lucius J. 1994. "Limits of Political Strategy: A Systematic View of the African American Experience." *American Political Science Review* 88 (March):1–13.

Barker, Twiley W., Jr., and Lucius J. Barker. 1987. "The Courts, Section 5 of the Voting Rights Act, and the Future of Black Politics." In *The New Black Politics: The Search for Political Power*, Second ed., ed. Michael Preston, Lenneal J. Henderson, Jr., and Paul Puryear. (White Plains, N.Y.: Longman). Pp. 59–75.

Beachler, Donald. 1995. "Racial Gerrymandering and Republican Gains in Southern House Elections." *The Journal of Political Science* 23 (annual):64–86.

Beauregard, Robert A. 1995. "If Only the City Could Speak: The Politics of Representation." In *Spatial Practices*, ed. Helen Liggett and David C. Perry. (Thousand Oaks, Calif.: Sage). Pp. 59–80.

Behr, Joshua G. 2000. "Black and Female Municipal Employment: A Substantive Benefit of Minority Political Incorporation?" *Journal of Urban Affairs* 22 (August):243–64.

Benenson, Itzhak, and Itzhak Omer. 2002. "Measuring Individual Segregation in Space: A Formal Approach and Case Study." In *Studies in Segregation and Desegregation*, ed. Itzhak Schness and Wim Osterndorf. (Burlington, Vt: Ashgate). Pp.11–38.

Berry, Barbara L., and Thomas R. Dye. 1979. "The Discriminatory Effects of At-Large Elections." *Florida State Law Review* 7 (annual):85–122.

Birch, Anthony Harold. 1971. *Representation.* New York: Preager.

Black Elected Officials: A Roster. Annual. Joint Center for Political Studies. New York: UniPublisher.

Blalock, Hubert M., Jr. 1979. *Social Statistics*, Second Ed. New York: McGraw Hill.

Blumstein, James F. 1995. "Racial Gerrymandering and Vote Dilution: *Shaw v. Reno* in Doctrinal Context." *Rutgers Law Journal* 26 (Fall):517–93.

Boal, F.W. 1976. "Ethnic Residential Segregation." In *Social Areas in Cities: Spatial Processes and Form*, ed. D. T. Herbert and R. J. Johnston. (New York: Wiley). Pp. 41–79.

Bork, Robert H. 1990. *The Tempting of America: The Political Seduction of the Law.* New York: Free Press.

Brace, Kimball, Bernard N. Grofman, Lisa R. Handley, and Richard G. Niemi. 1988. "Minority Voting Equality: The 65 Percent Rule in Theory and Practice." *Law and Policy* 10 (January):43–62.

Bratton, Kathleen. 2001. "Legislative Collaboration and Descriptive Representation." In *Representation of Minority Groups in the U.S.*, ed. Charles E. Menifield. (Lanham, Md.: Austin and Winfield). Pp. 289–311.

Brischetto, Robert R. 1998. "Latino Voters and Redistricting in the New Millennium." In *Redistricting and Minority Representation: Learning from the Past, Preparing for the Future*, ed. David A. Bositis. (Washington, D.C.: Joint Center for Political and Economic Studies and the University Press of America). Pp. 56–65.

Brouthers, Lance Eliot, and James S. Larson. 1988. "On Structure/Representation Linkages for Small Towns in the Deep South." *Journal of Urban Affairs* 10 (4):387–93.

Brown, Clyde. 1992. "The Electoral Risk of Redistricting: Evidence from the United States." *Electoral Studies* 11 (June):122–37.

Browning, Rufus P., Dale Rogers Marshall, and David H. Tabb, eds. 1997. *Protest is not Enough: The Struggle of Blacks and Hispanics for Equality in Urban Politics*, Second ed. Berkeley: University of California Press.

_______. 1997. *Racial Politics in American Cities.* New York: Longman.

Bullock, Charles S. 1975. "Redistricting and Congressional Stability, 1969–72." *The Journal of Politics* 32 (May):569–75.

_______. 1984. "Racial Crossover Voting and the Election of Black Officials." *The Journal of Politics* 46 (February):238–51.

_______. 1994. "Section 2 of the Voting Rights Act, Districting Formats, and the Election of African Americans." *The Journal of Politics* 56 (November):1098–105.

_______. 1995. "The Impact of Changing the Racial Composition of Congressional Districts on Legislators' Roll Call Behavior." *American Politics Quarterly* 23 (April):141–58.

_______. 1996. "Racial Composition of District Population and the Election of African-American Legislators." *Southeastern Journal of Political Science* 24 (April):611–28.

_______. 1999. "The Opening Up of State and Local Election Processes." In *American State and Local Politics: Directions for the 21st Century*, ed. Ronald E. Weber and Paul Brace. New York: Catham House.

Bullock, Charles S., and Harrell R. Rodgers Jr. 1975. *Racial Equality in America: In Search of an Unfulfilled Goal.* Pacific Palisades: Goodyear.

Bullock, Charles S., and Susan A. MacManus. 1990. "Structural Features of Municipalities and the Incidence of Hispanic Council Members." *Social Science Quarterly* 71 (December):665–81.

Burke, Christopher M. 1999. *The Appearance of Equality: Racial Gerrymandering, Redistricting, and the Supreme Court.* Westport: Greenwood.

Burton, Orville Vernon, Terrence R. Finnegan, Peyton McCrary, and James W. Loewen. 1994. "South Carolina." In *Quiet Revolution in the South: The Impact of the Voting Rights Act 1965–1990*, ed. Chandler Davidson and Bernard Grofman. (Princeton: Princeton University Press). Pp. 191–232.

Butler, Katharine Inglis. 1984. "Reapportionment, the Courts, and the Voting Rights Act: A Resegregation of the Political Process?" *University of Colorado Law Review* 56 (Spring):1–97.

Bybee, Keith J. 1998. *Mistaken Identity: The Supreme Court and the Politics of Minority Representation.* Princeton: Princeton University Press.

Cameron, Charles, David Epstein, and Sharyn O'Halloran. 1996. "Do Majority-Minority Districts Maximize Substantive Black Representation in Congress?" *American Political Science Review* 90 (December):794–812.

Campbell, David, and Joe R. Feagin. 1975. "Black Politics in the South: A Descriptive Analysis." *The Journal of Politics* 37 (February):129–62.

Canon, David T., Matthew M. Schousen, and Patrick J. Sellers. 1996. "The Supply Side of Congressional Redistricting: Race and Strategic Politicians, 1972–1992." *The Journal of Politics* 58 (August):846–62.

Carrol's Municipal/County Directory. Annual.

Carsey, Thomas M. 1995. "The Contextual Effects of Race on White Voting Behavior: The 1989 New York City Mayoral Election." *The Journal of Politics* 57 (February):221–28.

Charles, Camille Zubrinsky. 2001. "Socioeconomic Status and Segregation: African Americans, Hispanics, and Asians in Los Angeles." In *Problem of the Century*, ed. Elijah Anderson and Douglas Massey. (New York: Russell Sage Foundation). Pp. 271–89.

Charles, Guy-Uriel E. and Jason Roberts. 2001. "Determining 'Predominant Motive': Race, Redistricting, and the Supreme Court in North Carolina." Paper presented at the April 19–23, 2001, annual meeting of the Midwest Political Science Association, Chicago, Ill.

Chavez, Linda. 1992. "Hispanics, Affirmative Action, and Voting." *Annals of the American Academy of Political and Social Science* 523 (September):75–87.

Chervenak, Edward E., 1998. "1992 Congressional Redistricting in Louisiana: Drawing the Line on Race." *The Urban Lawyer* 30 (Winter):209–31.

Chrisman, Nicholas. 1997. *Exploring Geographic Information Systems.* New York: Wiley.

Clark, William V., and Peter A. Morrison. 1995. "Demographic Foundations of Political Empowerment in Multiminority Cities." *Demography* 32 (May):183–201.

Cohen, Jacob, and Patricia Cohen. 1983. *Applied Multiple Regression/Correlation Analysis for the Behavioral Science*, Second ed. Hillsdale, N.J.: LEA.

Conway, Margaret M. 1969. "Political Participation in Nonpartisan Local Elections." *Public Opinion Quarterly* 50 (Fall):425–30.

Conyers, James E., and Walter Wallace. 1976. *Black Elected Official: A Study of Black Americans Holding Government Office.* New York: Russel Sage Foundation.

Davidson, Chandler. 1979. "At-Large Elections and Minority Representation." *Social Science Quarterly* 60 (September):336–38.

_______. 1994. "The Recent Evolution of Voting Rights Law Affecting Racial and Language Minorities." In *Quiet Revolution in the South: The Impact of the Voting Rights Act 1965–1990*, ed. Chandler Davidson and Bernard Grofman. (Princeton: Princeton University Press). Pp. 21–37.

_______, ed. 1984. *Minority Vote Dilution.* Washington, D.C.: Howard University Press, Joint Center for Political Studies.

Davidson, Chandler, and George Korbel. 1981. "At-large Elections and Minority-Group Representation: A Re-Examination of Historical and Contemporary Evidence." *The Journal of Politics* 43 (November):982–1005.

Davis, Olethia. 1995. "Tenuous Interpretation: section 2 and 5 of the Voting Rights Act." *National Civic Review* 84 (Fall-Winter):310–23.

Dawson, Michael C. 1994. *Behind the Mule: Race and Class in African-American Politics.* Princeton: Princeton University Press.

Dawson, Michael C., Ronald E. Brown, and Richard Allan. 1999. "Racial Belief Systems, Religious Guidance, and African-American Political Participation." In *Black Electoral Politics*, ed. Lucius J. Baker. (New Brunswick: Transaction). Pp. 22–44.

DeLorenzo, Lisa C., Carol W. Kohfeld, and Linda Stein. 1997. "The Impact of Cross-Racial Voting on St. Louis Primary Election Results." *Urban Affairs Quarterly* 33 (September):120–33.

Denton, Nancy A., and Douglas S. Massey. 1988. "Residential Segregation of Blacks, Hispanics, and Asians by Socioeconomic Status and Generation." *Social Science Quarterly* 69 (December):797–817.

Directory of City and Policy Officials. Annual. National League of Cities, Center for Education and Information Resources. Washington, D.C.

Dixon, Robert G. 1982. "Fair Criteria and Procedures for Establishing Legislative Districts." In *Representation and Redistricting Issues,* ed. Bernard Grofman, Arend Lijphart, Robert B. McKay, Howard A. Scarrow. (Lexington: Lexington Books). Pp. 7–19.

Duncan, Otis D., and Beverly Duncan. 1955. "A Methodological Analysis of Segregation Indexes." *American Sociological Review* 20 (Summer):210–17.

Dunne, John R. 1993. "Remarks of [Assistant Attorney General] John R. Dunne." *Cardozo Law Review* 14 (April):1127–34.

Duverge, Maurice. 1951. *Party Politics and Pressure Groups.* London: Crowell.

Eagles, Munroe, Richard S. Katz, and David Mark. 1999. "GIS and Redistricting." *Social Science Computer Review* 17 (Spring):5–9.

Engstrom, Richard L. 1987. "District Magnitudes and the Election of Women to the Irish Dail." *Electoral Studies* 6 (August):123–32.

_______. 1994. "The Voting Rights Act: Disfranchisement, Dilution, and Alternative Election Systems." *PS* 12 (December):685–88.

_______. 1997. "Electoral Arrangements and Minority Political Incorporation." Paper presented at the Annual Meeting of the American Political Science Association, Washington, D.C.

Engstrom, Richard L., Stanley A. Halpin Jr., Jean A Hill, and Victoria M. Caridas-Butterworth. 1994. "Louisiana." In *Quiet Revolution in the South: The Impact of the Voting Rights Act 1965–1990,* ed. Chandler Davidson and Bernard Grofman. (Princeton: Princeton University Press). Pp. 103–35.

Engstrom, Richard L., and Michael D. McDonald. 1981. "The Election of Blacks to City Councils: Clarifying the Impact of Electoral Arrangements on the Seats/Population Relationship." *American Political Science Review* 75 (June):344–54.

_______. 1982. "The Underrepresentation of Blacks on City Councils: Comparing the Structural and Socioeconomic Explanations for South/Non-South Differences." *The Journal of Politics* 44 (November):1088–99.

_______. 1986. "The Effect of At-Large versus District Elections on Racial Representation in U.S. Municipalities." In *Electoral Laws and Their Political Consequences,* ed. Bernard Grofman and Arend Lipjphart. (New York: Agathon). Pp. 203–25.

_______. 1987. "The Election of Blacks to Southern City Councils: The Dominant Impact of Electoral Arrangements." In *Blacks in Southern Politics,* ed. Laurence W. Moreland, Robert P. Steed, and Tod A. Baker. (New York: Preager). Pp. 245–58.

Epstein, David, and Sharyn O'Halloran. 1999. "A Social Science Approach to Race, Redistricting, and Representation." *American Political Science Review* 93 (March):187–91.

_______. 1999. "Measuring the Electoral and Policy Impact of Majority-Minority Voting Districts." *American Journal of Political Science* 43 (April):367–95.

Eulau, Heinz, and Paul D. Karps. 1977. "The Puzzle of Representation: Specifying Components of Responsiveness." *Legislative Studies Quarterly* 2 (August):233–54.

Eulau Heinz, John C. Wahlke, William Buchanan, and Leroy C. Ferguson. 1959. "The Role of the Representative: Some Empirical Observations on the Theory of Edmund Burke" *American Political Science Review* 53 (September):742–56.

Flanigan, William H., and Nancy H. Zingale. 1998. *Political Behavior of the American Electorate*, Ninth ed. Washington, D.C.: Congressional Quarterly.

Foresman, Timothy W., ed. 1998. *The History of Geographic Information Systems: Perspectives from the Pioneers.* Upper Saddle River, N.J.: Prentice Hall.

Forest, Benjamin. 1995. "Taming Race: The Role of Space in Voting Rights Litigation." *Urban Geography* 16 (February):98–111.

_______. 1996. "Regionalism in Election District Jurisprudence." *Urban Geography* 17 (November):572–8.

Foster, Loren S. 1986. "Section 5 of the Voting Rights Act: Implementation of an Administrative Remedy." *Publius* 16 (Winter):17–24.

Freedman, David A., Stephen P. Klein, Jerome Sacks, Charles A. Smyth, and Charles G. Everett. 1991. "Ecological Regression and Voting Rights." *Evaluation Review* 15 (Fall):673–711.

Friedrich, Robert J. 1982. "In Defense of Multiplicative Terms in Multiple Regression Equations." *American Journal of Political Science* 26 (November):797–833.

Gay, Claudine. 2001. "The Effect of Black Congressional Representation on Political Participation." *American Political Science Review* 95 (September):589–602.

Gelman, Andrew, and Gary King. 1994. "Enhancing Democracy through Legislative Redistricting." *American Political Science Review* 88 (September):541–51.

Gierzynski, Anthony, and David Breaux. 1991. "Money and Votes in State Legislative Elections." *Legislative Studies Quarterly* 16 (May):203–17.

Giles, Michael W. 1977. "Percent Black and Racial Hostility: An Old Assumption Reexamined." *Social Science Quarterly* 58 (December):412–17.

Giles, Michael W., and Melanie A. Buckner. 1993. "David Duke and Black Threat: An Old Hypothesis Revisited." *The Journal of Politics* 55 (August):702–13.

_______. 1996. "Racial Threat Redux." *The Journal of Politics* 58 (November):1171–80.

Giles, Michael W., and Arthur S. Evans. 1985. "External Threat, Perceived Threat, and Group Identity." *Social Science Quarterly* 66 (March):50–66.

Glaser, James M. 1994. "Back to the Black Belt: Racial Environment and White Racial Attitudes in the South." *The Journal of Politics* 56 (February):21–41.

Golinger, Carolyn, ed. 1990. *Jigsaw Politics: Shaping the House after the 1990 Census.* Washington, D.C.: Congressional Quarterly.

Grofman, Bernard. 1985. "Criteria for Districting: A Social Science Perspective." *UCLA Law Review* 3377 (October):77–184.

Grofman, Bernard, and Lisa Handley. 1989a. "Black Representation: Making Sense of Electoral Geography at Different Levels of Government." *Legislative Studies Quarterly* 14 (May):265–79.

_______. 1989b. "Minority Population Proportion and Black and Hispanic Congressional Success in the 1970s and 1980s." *American Politics Quarterly* 17 (October):436–45.

_______. 1996. "Voting Rights in the 1990s: An Overview." In *Race and Redistricing in the 1990s*, ed. Bernard Grofman. (New York: Agathon). Pp. 69–79.

Grofman, Bernard, Lisa Handley, and Richard G. Niemi. 1992. *Minority Representation and the Quest for Voting Equality.* Cambridge: Cambridge University Press.

Grofman, Bernard, Arend Lijphart, Robert B. McKay, and Howard A. Scarrow, ed. 1982. *Representation and Redistricting Issues.* Lexington: Lexington Books.

Gronke, Paul, and J. Matthew Wilson. 1999. "Competing Redistricting Plans as Evidence of Political Motives: The North Carolina Case." *American Politics Quarterly* 27 (April):147–76.

Grose, Christian. 2001. "Black Legislators and White Districts, White Legislators and Black Districts: The Effect of Court-Ordered Redistricting on Congressional Voting Records in the South, 1993–2000." *The American Review of Politics* 22 (Summer):195–215.

Guinier, Lani. 1991a. "No Two Seats: The Elusive Quest for Political Equality." *Virginia Law Review* 77 (Winter):1413–514.

_______. 1991b. "The Triumph of Tokenism: The Voting Rights Act and the Theory of Black Electoral Success." *Michigan Law Review* 90 (Winter):1077–154.

_______. 1993. "The Representation of Minority Interests: The Question of Single Member Districts." *Cardozo Law Review* 14 (annual):1135–74.

_______. 1994. *The Tyranny of the Majority: Fundamental Fairness in Representative Democracy.* New York: Free Press.

Haeberle, Steven H. 1997. "Exploring the Effects of Single-Member Districts on an Urban Political System." *Urban Affairs Review* 33 (November):287–97.

Hagens, Winnett W. 1996. "The Politics of Race: The Virginia Redistricting Experience, 1991–1997." In *Race and Redistricing in the 1990s*, ed Bernard Grofman. (New York: Agathon). Pp. 315–42.

Hardy-Fanta, Carol. 1993. *Latina Politics, Latino Politics: Gender, Culture, and Political Participation in Boston.* Philedelphia: Temple University Press.

Harrison, Roderuck J., and Daniel H. Weinberg. 1992. Racial and Ethnic Residential Segregation in 1990." Paper presented for the Population Association of America meeting May 1992, Denver, Colorado.

Hawley, Albert. 1973. *Nonpartisan Elections and the Case for Party Politics.* New York: Wiley.

Heilig, Peggy, and Robert J. Mundt. 1983. "Changes in Representational Equity: The Effect of Adopting Districts." *Social Science Quarterly* 64 (June):393–97.

_______. 1984. *Your Voice at City Hall: The Politics and Policies of District Representation.* Albany: State University of New York Press.

Henry, Charles P. 1994. "Urban Politics and Incorporation: The Case of Blacks, Latinos, and Asian in Three Cities." In *Blacks, Latinos, and Asians in Urban America,* ed. James Jennings. (Westport, Conn.: Preager). Pp. 17–43.

Herring, Mary, and John Forbes. 1994. "The Overrepresentation of a White Minority: Detroit's At-Large City Council, 1961–1989." *Social Science Quarterly* 75 (June):431–45.

Hill, Rickey, and Brenda R. Reddix-Smalls. 2002. "The Limits of At-Large Elections: The Case of Florence County, South Carolina." In *Beyond the Color Line? Race, Representation, and Community in the New Century,* ed. Alex Willingham. (Brennan Center for Justice at NYU School of Law). Pp. 11–22.

Hodson, Timothy A. 1997. "Disappearing Constraints: Voting Rights and Gerrymandering in 2001." Unpublished paper presented at the 1997 Annual Meeting of the Western Political Science Association, Tucson, Arizona.

Hogan, Robert E. 2001. "The Influence of State and District Conditions on the Representation of Women in U.S. State Legislatures." *American Politics Research* 29 (January):4–24.

Hudson, David Michael. 1998. *Along Racial Lines: Consequences of the 1965 Voting Rights Act.* New York: Peter Lang.

Issacharoff, Samuel. 1992. "Polarized Voting and the Political Process: The Transformation of Voting Rights Jurisprudence." *Michigan Law Review* 90 (June):1833–91.

_______. 1997. "The Redistricting Morass." In *Affirmative Action and Representation:* Shaw v. Reno *and the Future of Voting Rights*, ed. Anthony A. Peacock. (Durham, N.C.: Carolina Academic Press). Pp. 201–20.

Issacharoff, Samuel, Pamela S. Karlan, Richard H. Pildes. 1998. *The Law of Democracy*, University Casebook Series. Westbury, N.Y.: Foundation.

Issacharoff, Samuel, and Richard H. Pildes. 1996. "No Place for Political Gerrymandering." *Texas Lawyer* (August):25.

Johnson, Nicole E. 2000. "Resources and the Representation of African Americans in the State Legislature." *Southeastern Political Review* 28 (March):151–63.

Johnson, Valerie C. 2002. *Black Power in the Suburbs: The Myth or Reality of African American Suburban Political Incorporation.* Albany: State University of New York Press.

Jones, Clinton B. 1976. "The Impact of Local Election Systems on Black Political Representation." *Urban Affairs Quarterly* 11 (March):345–56.

_______. 1979. "Demographic and Socioeconomic Correlates of Black Membership on City Councils." *South Atlantic Urban Studies* 4 (Annual):257–73.

Karnig, Albert K. 1976. "Black Representation on City Councils: The Impact of District Elections and Socioeconomic Factors." *Urban Affairs Quarterly* 12 (December):223–56.

_______. 1979. "Black Resources and City Council Representation." *The Journal of Politics* 41 (February):134–49.

Karnig, Albert K., and Susan Welch. 1979. "Sex and Ethnic Differences in Municipal Representation." *Social Science Quarterly* 60 (December):465–81.

_______. 1980. *Black Representation and Urban Policy.* Chicago: University of Chicago Press.

_______. 1982. "Electoral Structure and Black Representation on City Councils." *Social Science Quarterly* 63 (March):99–114.

Keech, William R., and Michael P. Sistrom. 1994. "North Carolina." In *Quiet Revolution in the South: The Impact of the Voting Rights Act 1965–1990*, ed. Chandler Davidson and Bernard Grofman. (Princeton: Princeton University Press). Pp. 155–89.

Kennedy, Randall. 1995. "Lani Guinier's Constituion." In *The American Prospect*, ed. Walter Dean Burnham. (Chatham House, New Jersey). Pp. 86–100.

King, Gary, John Bruce, and Andrew Gelman. 1995. "Racial Fairness Is Legislative Redstricting." In *Classifying by Race*, ed. Paul E. Peterson. (Princeton: Princeton University Press). Pp. 85–110.

Kousser, J. Morgan. 1999. *Colorblind Injustice: Minority Voting Rights and the Undoing of the Second Reconstruction.* Chapel Hill: University of North Carolina Press.

Kubin, Jeffrey C. 1997. "The Case for Redistricting Commissions." *Texas Law Review* 75 (annual):837–72.

Lakeman, Enid. 1974. *How Democracies Vote: A Study of Electoral Systems*, Fifth ed. London: Faber and Faber.

Latimer, Margaret K. 1979. "Black Political Representation in Southern Cities: Election Systems and Other Causal Variables." *Urban Affairs Quarterly* 15 (September):65–86.

Lee, Eugene C. 1960. *The Politics of Nonpartisanship: A Study of California City Elections.* Berkeley: University of California Press.

Lieberson, Stanley, and Donna Carter. 1982. "Temporal Change and Urban Differences in Residential Segregation: A Reconsideration." *American Journal of Sociology* 88 (Spring):296–310.

Lieske, Joel, and Jan William Hillard. 1984. "The Racial Factor in Urban Elections." *Western Political Quarterly* 37 (June):545–63.

Longoria, Thomas, Jr.. 1996. "White Attitudes toward Minority Electoral Districts: Minority Population Size, National Politics, and Local Policy." *Social Science Quarterly* 77 (December):877–87.

Lopez, Manual Mariano. "Patterns of Inter-ethnic Residential Segregation in the Urban Southwest." *Social Science Quarterly* 62 (January):50–63.

_______. 1999. "Racial Redistricting and African-American Representation: A Critique of 'Do Majority-Minority Districts Maximize Substantive Black Representation in Congress?'" *American Political Science Review* 93 (March):183–86.

Lublin, David, and Katherine Tate. 1995. "Racial Group Competition in Urban Elections." In *Classifying by Race*, ed. Paul E. Peterson. (Princeton: Princeton University Press) Pp. 245–61.

Lyons, W. E. 1969. "Legislative Redistricting by Independent Commissions." *Polity* 3 (Spring):428–59.

Lyons, W. E., and Malcom E. Jewell. 1988. "Minority Representation and the Drawing of Council Districts." *Urban Affairs Quarterly* 23 (March):432–47.

Macchiarola, Frank J., and Joseph G. Diaz. 1993a. "Decision Making in the Redistricting Process: Approaches to Fairness." *Journal of Legislation* 19 (Summer):199–222.

_______. 1993b. "The New York City Districting Commission: Renewed Opportunity for Participation in Local Government or Race Based Gerrymandering?" *Cardozo Law Review* 14 (Fall):1175–1218.

_______. 1993c. "Minority Political Empowerment in New York City: Beyond the Voting Rights Act." *Political Science Quarterly* 108 (Spring):37–57.

Mangione, Thomas W. 1995. *Mail Surveys: Improving the Quality*. Thousand Oaks, Calif.: Sage.

Mansbridge, Jane. 1999. "Should Blacks Represent Blacks and Women Represent Women? A Contingent 'Yes'." *The Journal of Politics* 61 (August):628–57.

Martin, David. 1996. *Geographic Information Systems: Socioeconomic Applications*, Second ed. New York: Routledge.

Massey, Douglas S. 1979. "Effects of Socioeconomic Factors on the Residential Segregation of Blacks and Spanish Americans in U.S. Urbanized Areas." *American Sociological Review* 44 (December):1015–22.

_______. 1994. "America's Apartheid and Urban Underclass: The Social Service Review Lecture." *Social Service Review* (December):471–85.

Massey, Douglas S., and Nancy A. Denton. 1987. "Trends in the Residential Seggregation of Blacks, Hispanics, and Asians: 1970–1980." *American Sociological Review* 52 (December):802–25.

_______. 1988. "Suburbanization and Segregation in U.S. Metropolitan Areas." *American Journal of Sociology* 94 (November):592–626.

_______. 1988b. "The Dimensions of Residential Segregation." *Social Forces* 67 (December):281–315.

_______. 1989. "Hypersegregation in U.S. Metropolitan Areas: Black and Hispanic Segregation along Five Dimensions." *Demography* 26 (August):373–91.

_______. 1993. *American Apartheid: Segregation and the Making of the Underclass.* Cambridge: Harvard University Press.

Massey, Douglas S., Andrew B. Gross, and Mitchell L. Eggers. 1991. "Segregation, the Concentration of Poverty, and the Life Chances of Individuals." *Political Science Research* 20 (Summer):397–420.

Massey, Douglas S., and Zoltan L. Hajnal. 1995. "The Changing Geographic Structure of Black-White Segregation in the United States." *Social Science Quarterly* 76 (September):526–42.

Mayhew, David R. "Congressional Representation: Theory and Practice in Drawing the Districts." In *Reapportionment in the 1970s*, ed. Nelson W. Polsby. (Berkeley: University of California Press). Pp. 249–92.

McDonald, Laughlin. 1989. "The Quiet Revolution in Minority Voting Rights." *Vanderbilt Law Review* 42 (May):1249–97.

_______. 1992. "The 1982 Amendments of section 2 and Minority Representation." In *Controversies in Minority Voting: The Voting Rights Act in Perspective*, ed. Bernard Grofman and Chandler Davidson. (Washington, D.C.: Brookings Institution). Pp. 66–84.

McDonald, Laughlin, Michael B. Binford, and Ken Johnson. 1994. "Georgia." In *Quiet Revolution in the South: The Impact of the Voting Rights Act 1965–1990*, ed. Chandler Davidson and Bernard Grofman. (Princeton: Princeton University Press). Pp. 67–101.

McDonald, Michael D., and Richard L. Engstrom. 1992. "Minority Representation and City Council Electoral Systems: A Black and Hispanic Comparison." In *Ethnic and Racial Minorities in Advanced Industrial Democracies*, ed. Anthony M. Messina, Luis R. Fraga, Laurie A. Rhodebeck, and Fredrick D. Wright. (Westport, Conn.: Greenwood). Pp. 127–42.

McKaskle, Paul L. 1995. "The Voting Rights and the 'Conscientious Redistricter.'" *University of San Franscico Law Review* 30 (Fall):1–94.

Meyer, Stephen Grant. 2000. *As Long as They Don't Move Next Door: Segregation and Racial Conflict in American Neighborhoods.* New York: Rowan and Littlefield.

Mollenkopf, John, David Olson, and Timothy Ross. 2001. "Immigrant Political Participation in New York and Los Angeles." In *Governing American Cities: Interethnic Coalitions, Competition, and Conflict*, ed. Michael Jones-Correa. (New York: Russell Sage Foundation). Pp. 17–70.

Moncrief, Gary F., and Joel A. Thompson. 1992. "Electoral Structure and State Legislative Representation: A Research Note." *The Journal of Politics* 54 (February):246–56.

Monmonier, Mark. 1995. *Drawing the Line: Tales of Maps and Cartocontroversy.* New York: Holt.

_______. 2001. *Bushmanders and Bullwinkles: How Politicians Manipulate Electronic Maps and Census Data to Win Elections.* University of Chicago Press.

Morrill, Richard L. 1987. "Redistricting, Region, and Representation." *Political Geography Quarterly* 6 (July):241–60.

Mosher, Frederick. 1969. *Democracy and Public Service.* New York: Oxford University Press.

Mundt, Robert J., and Peggy Helig. 1982. "District Representation: Demands and Effects in the Urban South." *The Journal of Politics* 44 (November):1035–48.

Municipal Yellow Book: Who's Who in the Leading City and County Governments and Local Authorities. Annual. New York: Monitor.

Murray, Richard, and Arnold Vedlitz. 1978. "Racial Voting Patterns in the South: An Analysis of Major Elections from 1960 to 1977 in Five Cities." *Annals of the American Academy of Political and Social Sciences* 439 (September):29–39.

National Association of Latino Elected and Appointed Officials. *National Roster of Hispanic Elected Officials.* Annual. Los Angeles: NALEO Education Fund.

Oliver, J. Eric, and Tali Mendelberg. 2000. "Reconsidering the Environmental Determinants of White Racial Attitudes." *American Journal of Political Science* 44 (July):574–89.

Orey, B. D'Andra. 2000. "Racism or Resentment: An Analysis of African Americans' Racial Attitudes toward Other African Americans." Paper presented at the Annual Meeting of the Southern Political Science Association, Atlanta, Ga., November.

O'Rourke, Timothy G. 1992. "The 1982 Amendments and the Voting Rights Paradox." In *Controversies in Minority Voting: The Voting Rights Act in Perspective*, ed. Bernard Grofman and Chandler Davidson. (Washington, D.C.: Brookings Institution). Pp. 85–113.

Overby, L. Marvin, and Kenneth M. Cosgrove. 1996. "Unintended Consequences? Racial Redistricting and the Representation of Minority Interests." *The Journal of Politics* 58 (May):540–50.

Parent, Wayne, and Paul Stekler. 1985. "The Political Implications of Economic Stratification in the Black Community." *Western Politics Quarterly* 38 (December):521–37.

Park, Robert E., Ernest W. Burgess, and Roderick D. McKenzie. 1925. *The City.* Chicago: University of Chicago Press.

Parker, Frank R. 1983. "The Results Test of Section 2 of the Voting Rights Act: Abandoning the Intent Standard." *Virginia Law Review* 69:715–764.

_______. 1995. "The Constitutionality of Racial Redistricting: *Shaw v. Reno*." *The District of Columbia Law Review* 3 (Spring):1–59.

Peterson, Paul E. 1995. "A Politically Correct Solution to Racial Classification." In *Classifying by Race*, ed. Paul E. Peterson. (Princeton: Princeton University Press). Pp. 3–17.

Pildes, Richard H. 1997. "Principled Limitations on Racial and Partisan Redistricting." *Yale Law Review* 106 (annual):2505–61.

_______. 2002. "Is Voting-Rights Law Now at War with Itself? Theories of Representation in Changing Political Circumstances." *University of North Carolina Law Review* 80 (annual):1518–71.

Pitkin, Hanna Fenichel. 1967. *The Concept of Representation.* Berkley: University of California Press.

Polinard, Jerry L., Robert D. Wrinkle, and Thomas Longoria Jr. 1991. "The Impact of District Elections on the Mexican American Community: The Electoral Perspective." *Social Science Quarterly* 72 (September):608–14.

Pomper, Gerald. 1966. "Ethnic and Group Voting in Nonpartisan Group Elections." *Public Opinion Quarterly* 50 (Spring):79–97.

Posner, Mark A. 1996. "Post-1990 Redistrictings and the Preclearance Requirement of section 5 of the Voting Rights Act." In *Race and Redistricing in the 1990s*, ed. Bernard Grofman. New York: Agathon. Pp. 80–117.

Rae, Douglas W. 2001. "Viacratic America: *Plessy* on *Foot v. Brown* on Wheels." *Annual Review of Political Science* 4 (annual):417–38.

Raskin, Jamin B. 1995. "Gerrymander Hypocrisy: Supreme Court's Double Standard." *The Nation* (February 6):167–68.

Reed, Judith. 1992. "Of Boroughs, Boundries and Bullwinkles: The Limitations of Single-Member Districts in a Multiracial Context." *Fordham Urban Law Journal* 19 (Spring):759–80.

Reeves, Keith. 1997. *Voting Hopes or Fears? White Voters, Black Candidates and Racial Politics in America.* New York: Oxford University Press.

Renner, Tari. 1999. "Election Processes and Minority Representation." In *Local Government Election Practices: A Handbook for Public Officials and Citizens*, ed. Roger L. Kemp. (Jefferson, N.C.: McFarland). Pp. 139–62.

Riemer, Neal, ed. 1967. *The Representative: Trustee? Delegate? Partisan? Politico?* Lexington, Mass.: D.C. Heath.

Robinson, Theodore P., and Thomas R. Dye. 1978. "Reformism and Black Representation on City Councils." *Social Science Quarterly* 59 (June):133–41.

Rogers, Mike, and Sally Friedman. 2000. "Dilemmas of Descriptive Representation: A Case Study of Two Majority-Minority Districts in 1990s New York." Paper presented at the Annual Meeting of the American Political Science Association, Washington D.C., September.

Rogerson, Peter A., and Zongxiang Yang. 1999. "The Effects of Spacial Population Distributions and Political Districting on Minority Representation." *Social Science Computer Review* 17 (Spring):27–39.

Rosenbaum, Emily. 1996. "The Influence of Race on Hispanic Housing Choices: New York City, 1978–1987." *Urban Affairs Review* 32 (November):217–43.

Rossiter, D. J., R. J. Johnston, and C. J. Pattie. 1997. "Redistricting and Electoral Bias in Great Britian." *British Journal of Political Science* 27 (July):466–72.

Roster of Black Elected Officials. Annual. Joint Center for Political and Economic Studies. Washington, D.C.

Rush, Mark E. 2000. *Does Redistricting Make a Difference? Partisan Representation and Electoral Behavior.* New York: Lexington Books.

Santos, Adolfo, and Carlos Huerta. 2001. "An Analysis of Descriptive and Substantive Latino Representation in Congress." In *Representation of Minority Groups in the U.S.*, ed. Charles E. Menifield. (Lanham, Md.: Austin and Winfield). Pp.58–75.

Sass, Tim R., and Stephen L. Mehay. 1995. "The Voting Rights Act, District Elections, and the Success of Black Candidates in Municipal Elections." *The Journal of Law and Economics* 38 (October):367–92.

Sauer, C. O. 1918. "Geography and the Gerrymander." *American Political Science Review* 12 (August):403–26.

Savage, David G. 1995. "The Redistricting Triangle." *State Legislatures* 21 (September):20–24.

Scarrow, Howard A. 2000. "Vote Dilution, Party Dilution, and the Voting Rights Act: The Search for 'Fair and Effective Representation.'" In *The U.S. Supreme Court and the Electoral Process*, ed. David K. Ryden. (Washington, D.C.: Georgetown University Press). Pp. 40–57.

Schaffner, Brian F., Mathew Streb, and Gerald Wright. 2001. "Teams without Uniforms: The Nonpartisan Ballot in State and Local Elections." *Political Research Quarterly* 54 (March):7–30.

Scher, Richard, Jon Mills, and John Hotaling. 1997. *Voting Rights and Democracy: The Law of Politics and Districting.* Chicago: Nelson-Hall.

Shelley, Fred M. 1994. "Geography, Territory, and Ethnicity: Current Perspectives From Political Geography." *Urban Geography* 15 (February):189–200.

Sigleman, Carol K., Lee Sigleman, Barbara J. Walkesz, and Michael Nitz. 1995. "Black Candidates and White Voters: Understaning Racial Bias in Political Perceptions." *American Journal Political Science* 39 (February):243–65.

Singh, Robert. 1998. *The Congressional Black Caucus: Racial Politics in the U.S. Congress.* Thousand Oaks, Calif.: Sage.

Sloan, L. 1969. "Good Government and the Politics of Race." *Social Problems* 17 (Summer–Spring):161–75.

Sørensen, Annemette, Karl Taeuber, and Lesslie J. Hollingsworth Jr. 1975. "Indexes of Racial Residential Segregation for 109 Cities in the United States, 1950–1970." *Sociological Focus* 8 (April):125–42.

Squire, Peverill, and Eric R. A N. Smith. 1988. "The Effect of Partisan Information on Voters in Nonpartisan Elections." *The Journal of Politics* 5 (February):169–91.

Stanley, Harold W. 1987. *Voter Mobilization and the Politics of Race: The South and Universal Suffrage, 1952–1984.* New York: Praeger.

Stewart, Joseph, Robert E. England, and Kenneth J. Meier. 1989. "Black Representation in Urban School Districts: From School Board to Office to Classroom." *Western Political Quarterly* 42 (June):287–305.

Strange, Rick G. 1989. "Application of Voting Rights Act to Communities Containing Two or More Minority Groups—When is the Whole Greater Than the Sum of the Parts?" *Texas Tech Law Review* 20 (annual):95–154.

Streb, Mathew J. 2002. *The New Electoral Politics of Race.* Tuscaloosa.: University of Alabama Press.

Sullivan, Kathleen M. 1997. "Representation of Racial Minorities." In *New Federalist Papers: Essays in Defense of the Constitution*, ed. Alan Brinkley, Nelson W. Polsby, and Kathleen M. Sullivan. (New York: W. W. Norton). Pp. 103–10.

Swain, Carol. 1993. *Black Faces, Black Interests: The Representation of African Americans in Congress.* Cambridge: Harvard University Press.

_______. 1998. "An Optimists View of Minority Representation." In *Redistricting and Minority Representation: Learning from the Past, Preparing for the Future*, ed. David A. Bositis. (Washington, D.C.: The Joint Center for Political and Economic Research and the University Press of America). Pp. 195–99.

Szarawarski, Alan E. 2000. "Do 'Appearances Matter'? Minority Representation and the Misplaced Focus of *Shaw v. Reno.*" Paper presented at the Annual Meeting of the American Political Science Association, Washington D.C., September.

Taebel, Delbert. 1978. "Minority Representation on City Councils: The Impact of Structure on Blacks and Hispanics." *Social Science Quarterly* 59 (June):142–52.

Taeuber, Karl E., and Alma F. Taeuber. 1965. *Negroes in Cities: Residential Segregation and Neighborhood Change.* Chicago: Aldine.

Teasley, C. E. 1987. "Minority Vote Dilution: The Impact of Election System and Past Discrimination on Minority Representation." *State and Local Government Review* 19 (Fall):95–100.

Thernstrom, Abigail M. 1987. *Whose Votes Count?* Cambridge: Harvard University Press.

Tobin, Gary A., ed. 1987. *Divided Neighborhoods: Changing Patterns of Residential Segregation.* Newbury Park, Calif.: Sage.

Turner, Marshall L., Jr., and Robert A. LaMacchia. 1999. "The U.S. Census, Redistricting, and Technology: A Thirty-Year Perspective." *Social Science Computer Review* 17 (Spring):16–26.

U.S. Census 1990. U.S. Department of Commerce, Economics, and Statistics, Bureau of the Census.

Vanderleeuw, James M. 1990. "A City in Transition: The Impact of Changing Racial Composition on Voting Behavior." *Social Science Quarterly* 71 (June):326–38.

Vedlitz, Arnold, and Charles A. Johnson. 1982. "Community Racial Segregation, Electoral Structure, and Minority Representation." *Social Science Quarterly* 63 (December):729–36.

Viteritti, Joseph P. 1994. "Unapportioned Justice: Local Elections, Social Science, and the Evolution of the Voting Rights Act." *Cornell Journal of Law and Public Policy* 4 (annual):199–271.

Voss, Stephen D. 1996. "Beyond Racial Threat: Failure of an Old Hypothesis in the New South." *The Journal of Politics* 58 (November):1156–70.

Voss, Stephen D., and David Lublin. 2001. "Black Incumbents, White Districts: An Appraisal of the 1996 Congressional Elections." *American Politics Research* 29 (March):141–82.

Walawender, Richard A. 1999. "At-Large Elections and Vote Dilution." In *Local Government Election Practices: A Handbook for Public Officials and Citizens*, ed. Roger L. Kemp. (Jefferson, N.C.: McFarland). Pp. 103–23.

Walton, Hanes. 1985. *Invisible Politics: Black Voting Behavior.* Albany: State University of New York Press.

Weber, Ronald E. 1995. "Redistricting and the Courts: Judicial Activism in the 1990s." *American Politics Quarterly* 23 (April):204–28.

Webster, Gerald R. 1997a. "The Potential Impact of Recent Supreme Court Decisions on the Use of Race and Ethnicity in the Redistricting Process." *Cities* 14 (January):13–19.

_______. 1997b. "Geography and the Decennial Task of Reistricting." *Journal of Geography* 96 (March/April):61–68.

_______. 2000. "Playing a Game with Changing Rules: Geography, Politics, and Redistricting in the 1990's." *Political Geography* 19 (January):141–161.

_______. 2002. "Rethinking the Role of Geographic Compactness in Redistricting." In *Beyond the Color Line? Race, Representation, and Community in the New Century*, ed. Alex Willingham. (Brennan Center for Justice at NYU School of Law). Pp. 117–33.

Welch, Susan. 1990. "The Impact of At-Large Elections on the Representation of Blacks and Hispanics." *The Journal of Politics* 52 (November):1050–76.

Welch, Susan, and Timothy Bledsoe. 1988. *Urban Reform and Its Consequences: A Study in Representation.* Chicago: University of Chicago Press.

Whitby, Kenny J. 1997. *The Color of Representation: Congressional Behavior and Black Interests.* Ann Arbor: University of Michigan Press.

White, John Kenneth, and Daniel M. Shea. 2000. "State and Local Parties: Mom-and-Pop Shops in the Information Age." *In New Party Politics: From Jefferson and Hamilton to the Information Age*. (Boston: Bedford/St.Martin's) Pp. 174–207.

White, Michael J. 1983. "The Measurement of Spacial Segregation." *American Journal of Sociology* 88 (Winter):1008–18.

_______. 1986. "Segregation and Diversity Measures in Population Distribution." *Population Index* 52 (Summer):198–221.

_______. 1987. *American Neighborhoods and Residential Differentiation*. New York: Russell Sage Foundation.

Wilkinson, Doris. 2000. Rethinking the Concept 'Minority': A Task for Social Scientist and Practioners." *Journal of Sociology and Welfare* 20 (March):115–32.

Williams, Justin C., Jr. 1995. "Political Redistricting: A Review." *Papers in Regional Science* 74 (Spring):13–39.

Williams, L. 1990. "White/Black Perceptions of the Electability of Black Political Candidates." *National Political Science Review* 2 (Spring):45–64.

Zax, Jeffrey S. 1990. "Election Methods and Black and Hispanic City Council Membership." *Social Science Quarterly* 71 (June):339–55.

Zellner, Dorothy M., and Margaret Carey. 1990. *And Before I'll Be a Slave: A Guide to Community-Based Voting Rights Litigation*. Voting Rights Project of the Center for Constitutional Rights. Hadley, Mass.: Common Wealth.

AUTHOR INDEX

SUBJECT INDEX